AIKIDO
for Life

AIKIDO
for Life

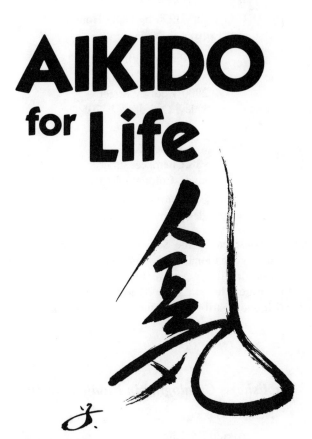

Gaku Homma

North Atlantic Books, Berkeley, California
Nippon Kan, Denver, Colorado

Aikido for Life
Copyright ©1990 by Gaku Homma
ISBN 1–55643–078–7
Published by
North Atlantic Books
2800 Woolsey Street
Berkeley, California 94705
and
Nippon Kan
988 Cherokee Street
Denver, Colorado 80204
Book design by Nippon Kan
Cover design by Paula Morrison

Aikido for Life is sponsored by the Society for the Study of Native Arts and Sciences, a nonprofit educational corporation whose goals are to develop an ecological and crosscultural perspective linking various scientific, social, and artistic fields; to nurture a holistic view of arts, sciences, humanities, and healing; and to publish and distribute literature on the relationship of mind, body, and nature.

Publisher's Cataloging in Publication Data

Homma, Gaku
Aikido For Life
Includes index
1. Aikido (Martial Arts)--Study and teaching
2. Psychology - Emotional Growth
3. Fitness, Health and Recreation
4. Philosophy--Budo, Zen, Shinto
I.Title

TO MY FIRST TEACHER

With thanks for having known you living in the Way.

O-Sensei, you once asked me,
    "Why haven't you practiced today?"
    "I had to cut the grass, Sensei," I replied.
    You smiled and said,
    "You can cut the grass any day,
    but this old man won't be around forever
    to teach you."

One beautiful afternoon you told me,
    "Go mail this package, and then we'll practice."
    You taught me suwari-waza
    in your everyday kimono.

I watched you on the train
    as we travelled to Headquarters in Tokyo.
    You bought a box lunch and some fruit
    for a little girl who sat across from you.

Later, at home in Iwama,
    in the quiet dojo
    after all the students had left,
    you sat facing the direction of Headquarters
    and expressed disappointment
    in the high-ranking students there.

Some men call you divine, a superior being,
    but I don't think that is right.
    You were a great martial artist,
    but at the same time,
    an ordinary, kind old man
    when not in the dojo.

That's why I try to follow,
    only because it is the way of Aiki,
    to which not a god, but a man
    opened the door.

Soon, your memorial day will come
    and I write this poem in gratitude.

Gaku Homma
Aikido NIPPON KAN

TABLE OF CONTENTS

Your Life is Your Dojo   1

Where is *Ki*?   5

I Didn't Knock on Your Door   11

Your Mind Moves Your Body   15

Your Enemy Is Yourself   19

There Are Two Of You   23

Take Off Your Work Hat   27

Open Your Hands   33

Things Have More Than One Side   37

It Is Natural To Fall   43

Your Partner Is Not Your Enemy   53

Your Partner Is A Mosquito   57

Learning From A Leaky Ceiling   61

Your Partner Is Not A Dummy   65

Artists Don't Start With The Eyes   69

Don't Judge A Still Picture   71

"Beep" Living   75

No Mistakes   79

Legal Size   83

I Won't Tell You   87

Scenery From The Window Of A Speeding Train   91

Eat Everything On Your Plate   95

Fried Rice   99

You Are $40   103

PREFACE

Seven years have passed since I first opened an Aikido *dojo* in Denver, Colorado. Today, I'm fortunate to have many excellent assistants, so I don't have much trouble communicating with people, but when I first came to the States, I had no way of expressing myself. I didn't speak English well. I didn't have much money either. I'm amazed to think back on the distance I have come. My English vocabulary was (and is) paper thin, and it was most difficult for me to express what I wanted to. But many of my students were patient with me and tried very hard to receive the message I was sending. I owe a great deal of my accomplishments today to the tolerant attitude of my students. I deeply appreciate the continuing support that they have given me.

Of course, there were many students who showed their dissatisfaction openly as if to say, "What is this Oriental guy trying to tell me?" I could not speak English fluently enough to explain things well. Because of this hardship, I have been forced to think of ways to express myself so that people understand what I'm saying, what I'm doing and what I'm trying to do. I could not use words to explain, but I could show what I meant. To act became my way of communicating, and my philosophy. According to this philosophy, I established my own method of instruction.

Today, I operate a non-profit cultural organization, NIPPON KAN. It is an organization formed to teach Japanese culture, perform cultural demonstrations and conduct seminars. Aikido is only one aspect of Japanese culture; I want people to understand that. I wish people to see Japan in a variety of aspects, and thus understand the background of Aikido.

The center was opened in the summer of 1982. To date, more than 5,000 people have participated in our courses and activities. The success of the center (where the main activity is training in the Japanese martial art of Aikido) is due to the students who continuously support our activities. The Center today is a US-Japanese cultural information exchange center, and TV stations and news firms not only from the Colorado area but also from Japan come to report on our activities.

There is a movement in Aikido called *tenkan* which is a turning of the body to check the situation around you. It is not only a practice of body placement, but also a change of viewpoint in relation to events surrounding you. One who practices *tenkan* must practice the application of the movement as well. I believe I have been applying Aikido movements in my living in a truly practical manner.

Every day is a new challenge to me, and I do my best in each current activity. When I finish a project, I look for another to work on. At the same time, I eat and drink well and sing very often. And a result is NIPPON KAN.

When I first came here I worked for a while as the manager of an apartment building in a dangerous part of town. I was shot at twice. I have worked as a door guard at rich folks' parties at the coldest time of the year. When we didn't have any food to eat, I collected greens from creek-sides to cook. I cleaned a building to make ends meet. All the hardships are now like a view from a train window. Those views are all past. NIPPON KAN developed during my struggle, and that was the most important thing to me.

I'm only afraid of becoming overly dependent upon Aikido. Aikido is my life, but I'm willing to accept the fact that it is not the only way to live. I will do anything to stay alive. For now, that is for the development of Aikido.

An instructor may be very good at Aikido, his techniques excellent, his rolls beautiful, his wrists so strong that stimulation techniques don't work on him. But What does all this mean? An ability to practice and teach techniques means very little unless a person has learned something from Aikido and applies what has been learned to daily life.

I don't belong to any Aikido organizations in the United States. To a martial artist, an organization can become an effective defense and may cause laziness. Once spoiled by the power that an organization gives, a person often begins to try to control others with that power. The organization can make him or her a weak martial artist.

A rose and a carnation are the same, yet different. They are both flowers, but different kinds of flowers. If you were seeing them together for the first time, you might want to point out the differences between them. Eventually, though, you may come to see that both are beautiful flowers. That state of mind is perhaps an approach to understanding Aikido as "Love and Harmony's Way." The founder, Morihei Ueshiba, said, "The beauty of this world is a family created by the gods." He had gone beyond differences to see the kinship of all things.

A martial artist is essentially a *Samurai*, and must, figuratively speaking, live alone. In order to live alone and survive, he must look for ways to avoid conflict with others. He must live in harmony with others to avoid conflict. Crushing an individual or a small organization using his organization's power is not the way for a martial artist. I welcome all students who come to my *dojo*, regardless of their affiliations. There are facilities at my *dojo* to house up to sixteen students while training here.

You might think that I, who wrote this book and preside over NIPPON KAN, must live a luxurious life. That is not so. I still live on the second floor of the *dojo*. I don't own a credit card. You know what it means to not own a credit card? For five years, I haven't taken a salary. I think of this way of life as training.

I wrote this book mainly for those who have just started Aikido training, but the book will also benefit those who have been training for many years as well as those who are in teaching positions now. The book follows the beginner's course of instruction at NIPPON KAN, but the beginner's course is not the only one we offer. We have children's classes and many advanced classes as well. Advanced classes are fast-paced, rigorous practice. In them, *bokken* (wooden sword) and *jo* (staff) movements are taught in relation to unarmed Aikido techniques. Going back to the roots of Aikido movements through weapons training is the specialty of my teaching. There are five volumes of video instruction on the subject. (Children and Aikido, in which the important contributions of Aikido training to children's emotional growth is discussed, is available as a booklet.)

Earlier, I mentioned the workings of modern Aikido society and its politics. I would like to point out in more detail that Aikido is essentially a gathering of people, and that there are very simple, human sides to Aikido. If people perceive Aikido as some sort of superpower, that notion places a generic instructor like myself in a very awkward situation.

In Aikido for Life, readers will find a simple definition of Aikido as a training of mind, breathing and body. The truth is that the harmony of mind, breathing and body cannot be achieved without training oneself. All beginning students in Aikido walk through similar stages of confusion and progress. I hope that this book will help clarify Aikido for all my fellow students.

Gaku Homma
April, 1988
Denver, Colorado

Chapter 1

Your Life is Your Dojo

The autumn sky was clear and blue, and the day, warm. It was the kind of day that draws people to walk and smell the deliciousness of the world before it passes into winter. Two children playing on a hill caught my attention. The first child held something in his hands, then swung one hand in a slow arc, releasing a trail of tiny rainbow-colored bubbles. He dipped into the soap again, and with a serious face, brought the dipstick to his face and blew a large, beautiful bubble. Then the two children began blowing bubbles at each other playfully. As they did, I watched carefully to see what would happen when the bubbles collided. Sometimes, only one of the bubbles would break. Sometimes, both were broken. Once in a while, the bubbles would stick together, yet remain separate bubbles. But the most fascinating to me was when the bubbles would join, become one, and be lifted into the air together.

In watching the children, I realized something important . Those delicate bubbles, as they floated out into the sky, became different shapes and forms - but they all had come from the same material. How clearly, it seemed to me, are both life and the martial arts related to the innocent play of children.

The way of Aikido can be found in the story of the bubbles, especially in the instance where two bubbles join and become one when they meet. A child with a determined face patiently blows a beautiful bubble until it becomes whole and floats alone. Human life can be thought of in the same manner. We are all nurtured by parents until we are whole enough to stand alone. Like the bubbles, we grow into many shapes and forms, yet we are all essentially the same.

Morihei Ueshiba, the founder of Aikido, has said, "Aikido is the way of non-violence, blending and harmony." Aikido movements do not meet force with force. They are not like the bubbles that hit one another in a way that causes both to break. Aikido movement is blending, harmonizing, like two bubbles that meet in such a way that they become one.

In practicing Aikido, all aikidoists - beginners and instructors alike - need to find the heart of Aikido and integrate it into their daily life. Our days are filled with hard work, obligations and responsibilities. How many hours can you spare for Aikido practice? Two or three at most. Can you do that everyday? Not realistically. For most, only a small part of life is spent in the physical practice of Aikido.

An instructor of martial arts is called a *shihan*, meaning "one who sets an example." For many years I have challenged myself to find the true meaning of being a *shihan*. An instructor may be very good at Aikido, with excellent techniques, beautiful rolls and wrists so strong that stimulation techniques have no effect. But what does this all mean? An ability to practice and teach techniques means very little unless a person has learned something from Aikido and applies what has been learned to daily life. It is a *shihan's* responsibility to show how the philosophy of his or her martial art can be applied in daily life. He or she should not be a teacher only in the *dojo*, or a teacher of physical techniques alone.

For one thing, practice is not limited to the confines of a square matted area. If we open our minds and take a moment to look at Aikido from a slightly different angle, we can see that Aikido practice is everywhere, all of the time. If we start from this point we can search for a true Aikido mind. It is important not to believe blindly in one set definition of what Aikido is. Unquestioned acceptance concerns me.

There is a saying among Zen priests: *"Hobo kore dojo,"* which translated means, " your life is your *dojo*." As your life changes from moment to moment, you must be flexible in observing it in order to blend and be in harmony with it.

During Aikido practice, a lot of questions naturally arise, especially for those in an instructor's position. Interestingly, beginners ask questions that are so simple they become the most difficult to answer. For example, in practice, the Aikido movement begins when a strike or grab is initiated. From an instructor's point of view this seems obvious. But a beginning student once asked me: "What happens if your partner lets go of your hand in the middle of an attack?"

My answer was, "just laugh, and start again."

Yet this simple question was the subject of daily thought for me for many years. The answer, like a Zen koan, was not arrived at easily. Beginning instructors might advise using the opening to counterattack. But to answer with laughter and cooperation, and not to use the opportunity to counter takes a stronger heart and mind.

Another student asked me: "Why do we bow to the front?" Again, a very simple question with a seemingly simple answer.

"We bow in respect to the founder," I said. This is true. But in actuality, what we are bowing to is not the founder, but an image in a photograph. Upon realizing this, I have tried to find a new answer. Still I am thinking . . .

One way to look at it is that behind the wall is the landlord's office, where he might be sitting at his desk. On 365 days a year, we bow serenely in his direction - and even give him our monthly dues. It might certainly be interpreted that we are praying to our landlord!

Yet, we bow. Many people bow toward the founder's picture - and the wall it hangs on - innocently and with a good heart every day. Let's think how this wall affects our daily life.

There are many "walls" before us in our daily lives. These walls represent barriers or problems that we need to face. By greeting these walls the way we bow to that wall in the *dojo*, we can more likely find a way to step over them. And even when we cannot get over a particular wall, we can learn from it. If you can graciously accept these walls a teachers, then you life becomes your *dojo*. Looking at life this way helps you attain a very calm, wide view of the world.

This is " *hobo kore dojo*." Your life is your *dojo*. If you can see life in this manner, a lot of frustration and suffering can be released, like a bubble, to float away gently. This is Aikido's meaning: love and harmony's way. This life is yours to create.

Aikido is everywhere, if you can see.

I fear most the idea of trying to separate Aikido from life: seeking answers only in the *dojo* - becoming dependent on a rigid definition of Aikido. Aikido is not a superpower. This is an illusion. When writing the second draft for the second chapter, "Where is *Ki*?" many of my assistants were worried that my words were too strong and might offend others. But to hold true to Nippon Kan's teachings, I cannot ignore the points I make about *ki* in that chapter. It is important to try to dispel the illusions that have arisen. Likewise, Doshu Kisshomaru Ueshiba, the founder's son, states in many of his publications as well that one does not find *ki* by adopting another's definition blindly. Only through daily practice (*gyo*) - inside and outside the dojo - can one find understanding (*etoku*).

Possibly a few will criticize me. This I understand.

Chapter 2

Where is Ki?

Many people think that the most important idea in Aikido is *ki*. Well, please let me see *ki*. What is its color, shape and weight? Where is it? Believers in *ki* cannot answer these questions. They try to explain it using words they once read in a book. I ask, "Show it to me, please." Some of them say, "It is the unified energy of mind and body." Again I ask, "Please, let me see it." Then they admit, "You can't see it. *Ki* has no shape."

The word *ki* is made of two letters, 'k' and 'i' nothing more. Of course, you know how difficult it is to understand something that can only be imagined. Some try to describe this thing that doesn't exist by letting their explanations drift into the realm of mystery. The mystery of *ki* has been deceiving many students.

"Well, what is the essence of Aikido?" When someone tries to answer this question you hear "*ki*" this and "*ki*" that. You hear about the "unbendable arm" and "unliftable body," fruits of hard practice and sweat in Aikido training, not of *ki* theory. Practice with a *bokken* (wooden sword) every day, and you will have unbendable arms. It is not magic. But what if your strong arm which was built by lifting weights was bent? You weigh twice as much as the demonstrator, but he lifted you easily? Of course, because he knew how to bend and lift. These tricks are performed at demonstrations as a sort of advertising. Impressive and mysterious feats will naturally attract students who would like to learn to perform them. I am not condemning this practice out of hand, but I do feel it is misleading to present Aikido as a series of magic tricks.

In one popular demonstration, two big guys try to lift the demonstrator by the arms. In their first attempt, the men can easily lift the demonstrator, and he tucks his legs so it seems to the spectators that he is lifted really high. On the second try, they cannot lift him at all! Amazing! But there is a slight difference in the demonstrator's stance; he is controlling the leverage the two men can exert by repositioning them awkwardly. If the men simply relax, squat down, and lift the demonstrator with the power in their legs, he can be easily lifted. The trick takes some skill, perhaps, and a sense of showmanship, but no mysterious powers are involved. Even the highest ranking masters can be lifted in this way (Figure 2-1).

Figure 2-1: Aikido demonstrations don't show off magical powers as much as an understanding of the laws of physics.

In another demonstration, the demonstrator has a member of the audience sit on the floor. This person is easily pushed over backwards. Then, the demonstrator sits and has several people line up one behind the other and attempt to push him over, but they can't. Observe very carefully the position of his hands. He places them under the first person's elbows, directing all the force that comes from the first person upward and beyond him, thus making it impossible to push him over. If the first person could push squarely, it wouldn't be hard for just one person to push the demonstrator over (Figure 2-2).

Figure 2-2: This demonstration looks magical - but it's really not.

Another example is the "unbendable arm." Strong-looking men try unsuccessfully to bend a master's arm. First the demonstrator picks one man to try, the demonstrator appearing to resist strongly, and finally allowing the man to succeed. He explains, - "without *ki*, that is what happens." Then with *ki*, he lets a few people hold on to his arm. Please stop here and think: how many people can hold on to a two-foot long arm at once in a way that allows them to effectively apply pressure in the same direction? And do they have enough space to use their full power (Figure 2-3)? There isn't enough room around the arm of the demonstrator, that's for sure. In fact, the men get in each other's way. The demonstrator is perfectly aware of these facts, but he says that what has happened is because of *ki*. It is not hard to dazzle an audience if they don't know the trick, and they leave thinking that *ki* is a great and mysterious power.

Figure 2-3: Is it really an "unbendable" arm?

One method of teaching *Aiki* exercise uses a similar approach. This simple exercise is done on five counts with the students standing. The instructor stops the exercises by saying, "Now I will check the extension of your *ki*." He then goes around pushing students over. The instructor lectures about *ki*, then repeats the pushing. This time the students don't move. The instructor praises the students, since they are beginning to understand *ki*. It is so simple to push in a direction that forces the student to move, then to push in a direction that only stabilizes the student. The existence of *ki* is "proved" by verbal skill, showmanship and tricks. Such deceptive methods were used frequently in traditional secretive Japanese Buddhism, Shinto, and martial arts, both to gain more followers and to intimidate rivals. Super-natural or extraordinary illusions were created by tricks to impress spectators.

People tend to be drawn easily to special powers as if they will provide a simple solution to life's problems. But think a moment. Do our lives really improve by becoming dependent on a special power? Or is it perhaps a sign of laziness? In the past, many masters walked paths of discipline and severity to establish their schools of martial arts. It took tremendous effort and dedication to reach the point where they could truly be called "master". Knowing that, how could an honest person go around teaching and theorizing about Aikido as if it could be summed up in so many words? As you are aware, there are some things we cannot achieve without hard work and a lot of sweat. You can never reach enlightenment by seeking easy answers.

There is a story I sometimes use in my classes as an example. It is the story of the "Aikido Baby." One day a baby was born, and was named "Aikido." As the baby grew his diapers were changed and he was fed. He cried without consideration for the time. Of course the baby was adorable and was loved, but he also got sick inconveniently now and then. As he grew older, he went through a period of resistance, started driving a car, found a girlfriend and got married. This is how any baby grows up to be an adult and a responsible member of society. No child is born grown-up, a responsible citizen. The process of growing up is very important. Of course, it was hard work raising the Aikido baby to become a fine adult, but we learned to find joy, happiness and hope in addition to the hardships.

The same is true in Aikido training or in any other discipline. You cannot expect the end result instantly, without the process. Many students and instructors today focus too much on results, under the impression that learning Aikido means learning a special power. The misconceptions surrounding Aikido must be dispelled so that students may start in the right place. I would like you to become aware of the reality of Aikido.

In order to turn a page in this book you must want to turn the page, and command your hands to do so. In order to eat, you must feel hungry and move your hands to get food from the table to your mouth. If you need something you must go and get it. And if you want training, you must work hard. Perhaps someone could feed you and anticipate and fulfill many of your other needs, but some things you must do for yourself.   ~~~

Chapter 3

I Didn't Knock on Your Door

I have taught a course called *"Introduction to Aikido"* many times at NIPPON KAN. Each class lasts an hour and a quarter, and a course consists of twelve classes. Thirty students participate in each course; there are three sections each term. Every six weeks, I repeat the same things in these introductory courses. Instructing a hundred beginners every six weeks is a kind of - training more valuable in some ways than actually working out. How *ikkyo* is done, or how *kotegaeshi* should be practiced become minor details.

Figure. 3-1: What is *your* image of martial arts?

Beginning students bring a number of images of martial arts to the Aikido *dojo*. Their understanding of Aikido at this early stage is reflected in the way they dress. Some wear martial arts uniforms with various patches from different schools. Some wear brand new Aikido uniforms, but with the jackets crossed incorrectly, right lapel over left. Some wear T-shirts and shorts, or sweatpants and sweatshirts. Some come in slacks and dress shirts, or jeans and work shirts, and I must not forget to mention those in leotards and legwarmers!

I begin the first class of a beginner's course with this statement: "I didn't knock on your door and talk you into joining this class." I tell these beginners that I didn't walk around their neighborhoods handing out our newsletter, asking them to join my classes. It all started when each of them picked up our newsletter, looked through it and decided to join the course. "You filled out the registration form, wrote a check, put a stamp on the envelope and mailed it to us," I say.

I wish to reinforce in their minds the fact that they are responsible for their decisions and for carrying them out. I understand that some of us don't like the idea of being responsible for our decisions and actions, but nonetheless we are.

Figure 3-2: Nobody dragged you into the dojo!

Continuing with my introductory speech, I ask them to open the yellow pages sometime to the martial arts section. It is found under "K", right after "Junk" and before "Kennels". This doesn't give a positive image of martial arts, but since "Karate" and "Kung fu" are better known, these words are used as common rather than proper nouns. Years ago, martial arts were listed under "J" for "Judo" so it is changing with the times.

Looking through the Yellow Pages list of martial art schools is like walking through a shopping center decorated for Christmas shoppers. Even questionable martial arts schools pose themselves for interested potential students, and solicit telephone calls and visits. Aikido is listed there as well. It is like shopping at a department store. Samples are available right there, so you can decide which one to try. At a shoe store, for example, you look through the stock and choose a design to satisfy your taste, ask a sales clerk to bring out your size, and you try them on. You like them and pay the price. Then you wear them for a little while, and if you think they do not quite fit as you hoped, you throw them away or put them in a closet to be thrown away later. Martial arts training is very similar for some people. If you don't get the result you were looking for right away, you quit and look for another. Many beginners come to my *dojo* with this kind of attitude.

Figure 3-3: Some people want instant success. To truly appreciate any martial art, you must be prepared to practice for many years.

Just the opposite attitude isn't rare either. Many beginners are fascinated by what martial arts training supposedly gives them and make a decision based on dubious preconceptions. Misled by the idea of *ki*, a woman may come to believe that *ki* is what's missing in her life. Or a man may come to the *dojo* thinking that he will learn ways to destroy everything that comes in his direction, so that he will be "number one." Many types of people gather together in the training hall on the first day of my Aikido introductory class.

There are certain characteristics in individuals who choose to try Aikido. There are many martial arts schools listed in the yellow pages, and the more there are, the less chance there is that any given individual will choose Aikido. But my new students did pick Aikido out of all the choices. Most of them want something out of Aikido and judged that they could not get it from another martial art. They are goal-oriented individuals, I hope. I want them to reconfirm the fact that THEY chose to enroll in the course. I didn't knock on their door to bring them here.

They went through the process of searching through the yellow pages or other printed information, asking themselves "which shall I choose?" or saying to themselves, "maybe this is good for me" or "let's call and find out how much it is." There may have been friends or family members encouraging them, but the final decision was theirs. A fancy ad in the yellow pages cannot make a decision for you. If you show the "Karate and other martial arts" section of the yellow pages to someone who has no interest in martial arts training, he will not feel any desire to call.

At the very beginning of Aikido training, I like my students to be aware that they come because they want to. You decided to come. This means that the mind acted first, and the body followed. It is the mind that made the body come here. Nothing else could have done that. If your mind is at home watching TV or drinking beer, and your body alone is here taking Aikido lessons, you have a serious problem! Each student needs to understand this before going on to the next step.   ~~~

Chapter 4

Your Mind Moves Your Body

Your mind gives commands to your body to do or not to do things. Unless you are hypnotized or drugged, it is not possible for you to attack someone without a conscious awareness of doing so. All actions that you take - good or bad - are the result of your decisions, because your mind commands your body. Many people have devoted their lives to the training of their minds, expending a great deal of time and effort. For many priests and martial artists, life is dictated by training of the mind.

Perhaps it will not appeal to you if I tell you that the goal of Aikido training is to understand your mind. You may never accomplish this. Therefore, try to see Aikido training as a way of understanding how important your mind is, as a way of becoming aware of the fact that your mind controls you.

Aikido training is the training of the mind. The mind is a difficult object, as incomprehensible as *ki*. We don't know where it is, or what color or shape it is. We don't know how much it weighs. We know the mind is important, but we have never seen it. In the two cultures, Japanese and American, our eyes and ears are located in the same place, so the location of the mind should be the same. But it is different. When I ask you where your mind is, you, as an American, point to your head. But in Japan, we point to our heart. Even the location of the mind differs in these two cultures.

Comparatively speaking, it is easy to train your body. You can go out and jog around a park, or go to a gym and pump iron. After a workout, you can stand in front of a mirror and see the progress. But training the mind does not work so easily. It would be much easier if you could take your mind to a park, take it out of your body and tell it to jog around the park. When done, you would pick up your mind, dust it off, remove its little running shoes, and put it back in its original position. Of course this is not possible!

Do you know your mind's best friend? It is breathing. There are two aspects of breathing: inhalation and exhalation. I left out the third one, "stop," but we don't need to practice that! When you are surprised, you inhale. After a long day of work, when you get home, you sit on your couch and exhale. When you are angry, you are breathing at the top of your chest. When you are confused or troubled, you exhale and inhale in short, weak spurts. If you pay attention, you will be amazed at how breathing reflects a person's mind and its condition. I don't intend to give medical explanations for all this, but will discuss it from an Aikidoist's point of view.

Naturally, breathing almost unconsciously reflects your mind. It is also something you can consciously control. You can hold your breath - for a short time. You can change the intervals of inhalation and exhalation at will. For example, before getting up on a stage or platform to give a speech, many people take a few deep breaths. Or after getting upset by an annoying driver zooming by you, you may exhale deeply to calm yourself down. Many of us do these things without actually being aware of them; they are unconscious acts, which is an interesting point. Try observing your breathing closely. When you are excited, how do you breathe? When you are depressed, how do you breathe? Then try breathing out deeply when you are excited, and try inhaling strongly when you are depressed or tired. Your breathing is done unconsciously for the most part, but you also know that you can control it. In turn, if you train your breathing with conscious effort, you can influence your mind.

The breathing patterns mentioned are effective even when done unconsciously. If you will the conscious mind to take control, the effects will be even greater.

Now that you have some idea of the relation between your mind and your breathing, we can talk about the actual practice of breathing. You breathe 24 hours a day, 7 days a week, non-stop, so any time is a good time for practice. But as I mentioned earlier, we all breathe unconsciously. It is done so naturally that we rarely pay attention to it. It wouldn't be productive to try to practice 24 hours a day, nor would it be practical. So many things are going on around us that we cannot pay attention to our breathing at all times. As soon as we wake up, we have to be thinking about what to do and what has to be done, so that we can maintain our lives. Working people have to get ready to go to work, carry out their duties, think about what to eat, plan what to do after work, and so on. Homemakers have a lot of work to keep up their household standards. Children have to get ready to go to school, cope with peer pressure and play with friends.

The only time we become aware of breathing is when we cannot do it smoothly, like during a headcold when our noses are stuffed, when we choke on food or smoke, or stay underwater a little too long. In reality, we just don't have a lot of time to concern ourselves with the relationship between our minds and breathing. So, what we must do is to find a way to integrate our breathing training into our daily activities.

Try this: open your hands and raise your arms. Naturally, you inhale with this action. Now, bend your body and curl up. You naturally exhale with this. Repeat the exercise a few times. Then, try it with the breathing reversed. Make fists and raise your arms while exhaling, then curl up while inhaling. Do you feel the difference? In the first exercise, the breathing and the actions matched and felt right. And in the second exercise, you felt awkward or uncomfortable, right? Try the same exercises in front of a mirror and you will actually see the difference.

Whether opening the hands or making fists, stretching your body or curling up, different breathing gives different feelings. When your body movements match your breathing, you feel good - and vice versa. When your body is stretched open, you inhale, and when your body shrinks down, you exhale. It's like an air bellows. When you breathe properly with matching body movements you gain energy. When you breathe in harmony with your body actions, then your energy flares up as if a fuel (called "mind") were igniting.

I believe these relationships pertain to any sport, martial art or body movement. The goal of Aikido training is to find and coordinate the relationships of mind, breathing and body movement. To do this, practice movements with perfectly matched breathing; that is training for the mind. Not by sitting in a meditative lotus position and watching your breathing, but by proper breathing with movement can you find a calm and clear mind. Learning a martial art, in which a moment of looseness can mean a fatal mistake, is training for the mind.

All this has something in common with today's lifestyles. At work and in business, the slightest looseness can result in a costly mistake or other damage to you and your company. It is not the same as meditation in remote mountains, where there is nothing to worry about besides searching for the mind. With that type of training, you are likely to develop a headache as soon as you return to your normal life. (Of course, we don't carry swords around downtown just because we are in training. We don't have to hop onto our desks and begin meditating, either.) Aikido training is conducted with the idea that your daily life is your training. Thus you need not be selective of location or time.

The mind moves the body. Easily said. But without a way to connect the two, you don't exist. If you doubt my words, try to stop breathing. The harder you exercise, the harder you have to breathe. When the two match, it gives a good feeling. It is a feeling you will achieve through a long period of conscious training in breathing and body movements. This is fundamental to Aikido training: harmony among movements, breathing and mind.   ~~~

Chapter 5

Your Enemy Is Yourself

When you begin Aikido or any other Japanese martial art, two Japanese customs await you. One is "rei", a bow from either a sitting or a standing position. From a sitting position, place both hands palm down on the floor in front of you and bow deeply. From a standing position, bend forward from the waist. In general, we bow as a group before and after class, and individually when greeting or thanking fellow students and instructors, or when entering and leaving the *dojo*. We use the sitting bow for *taijutsu* (unarmed techniques) and the standing bow when practicing with *bokken* (sword) or *jo* (staff or walking stick).

The second custom is "*seiza*," kneeling while sitting back on the feet. *Seiza* is an uncomfortable position not only for American beginners but even for advanced students. Some instructors force their students to sit in this position, telling them that they cannot learn anything else until they are able to sit in *seiza*. I don't insist that my students, except for black belts, sit in *seiza*. Being able to sit in *seiza* means that the person's knee and ankle joints are limber enough to let circulation continue in the lower legs. As such, it is a part of training but not a requirement.

Once, a beginning student asked a master the reason he had to sit in *seiza*. The teacher's reply was, "That is the way it is done," and he made the student sit in *seiza* for a long time as if punishing him for asking such a question. "That is the way" is not an explanation. If you sit in *seiza* for a long time, your feet will go to sleep, so you cannot get up or move around easily for a while. It doesn't make sense to put students of martial arts in a position where they cannot move around easily. In my classes, when I expect my speech or explanation to be long, I tell students to sit comfortably. I would much prefer that the students listen to me and understand what I'm saying rather than lose their concentration because their feet are becoming numb! The only times that I expect all students to sit in *seiza* are briefly when we begin and end a class, before and after a demonstration of a technique to be worked on, and when the students enter and leave the *dojo*.

It is interesting to look at the practice of *seiza* from an historical point of view. To a host surrounded by many visitors, having his guests sit in *seiza* is the safest arrangement, since an attack from *seiza* position is awkward. Originally, this position was forced upon people by those in power to assure their security. The custom had its roots in distrust, but eventually became a way to show courtesy and mutual good intentions, much as in the West one shakes hands with the right (weapon) hand as a sign of friendship. When you sit in *seiza* you are expressing peaceful intentions, thus communicating respect. Therefore, I don't believe *seiza* is something that should be forced. *Seiza* is a gesture of respect in a framework of custom. Those who have respect for each other sit in *seiza* as an exchange of courtesy.

One day I had three visitors observing my class. They were students of Aikido, but not from my school. They came into the *dojo* and sat in *seiza*. That's good etiquette. Then I had my assistant tell them to make themselves comfortable. They didn't move. Ten minutes later, I sent the same message. No change. Their concentration became scattered soon after that. They should have taken my suggestion earlier and sat in a comfortable position. They sat in *seiza* through the entire class, and couldn't move normally for a while afterward. Later, they left a dollar each as an observation fee. What kind of etiquette is that? Watching them, I could picture their teacher as one who emphasizes style rather than practicality, wrapping rather than content.

When you are expected to sit in *seiza*, think of it as a warm-up exercise, stretching your knee and ankle joints. Soon you will become more flexible and won't feel apprehensive about it. Whether you can do it or not is up to you. If you decide you cannot do it without trying, then you will never be able to. With this kind of attitude, you won't be able to learn much from Aikido, either. View it as an exercise for your legs, not a way to polish an apple for your instructor.

Overcoming yourself is sometimes like deceiving yourself, for martial arts training requires great discipline. Many times in the course of training, you will reach a point of thinking you cannot do any more, cannot go further. When that happens, you have to tell yourself that you can. It is like lying to a part of yourself so that you can go on. This will extend the limits of your martial arts training. Doing an exercise, such as *ukemi* (breakfalls) fifty times in succession is tough work for anybody. But if you tell yourself that you can do more and then actually do it, you will be a better Aikidoist for it. You might say that this is a positive use of self-deception.

Daily life is filled with compromises. Compromise is also a way of lying to yourself. If we lived our lives in such a way that each of us did exactly as he or she pleased, then there would be chaos. Consideration for fellow human beings forces us to compromise our own self-interest, follow rules, and observe courtesy and etiquette. Many times, considerate behavior does not quite get us what we really want. Although we understand the reasons for civil behavior, there is a part of us which must be deceived in order to live among others.

One very cold winter day, wearing only a single-layer Aikido uniform, many of my Aikido students and I jogged in a park near our *dojo*. It was 4 degrees (F.) outside, and we couldn't stay still, or our limbs would start hurting. "I don't want to do this," the true self says. "I told them I'd join them, so I'd better," the conscience says. It becomes a struggle within yourself. Part of you wants to say "no way," and yet another part says, "I can do it." That is the nature of training. A little more, a littlé faster or a little better - that is the goal of training. That is how the advanced students learned to sit in *seiza* for longer periods of time.

"A little more" is a very important attitude. Without it, there can be no improvement. When you think "this is my limit," and you quit, you will never go beyond that point.

There are no tournaments in Aikido. This is because competition is not necessary. In a tournament, the situation is very limited. It takes place within a ring with two contenders fighting against one another. To win a match, one opponent must be beaten; the winner then jumps around in the ring waving to excited spectators. They may remember the fight, but who will think about the fighters tomorrow?

Figure 5-1: Your own worst enemy and your own best friend is the person you greet each morning in your own mirror.

In Aikido we seek a broader battlefield, one not limited by feelings of competition. Instead, the enemy is within ourselves. Life is a continuous battle within. For each of us, the self is both the closest friend and the toughest enemy (Fig.5-1). It is very difficult to appease that enemy or to be friends with it. The self is the hardest partner to control. How could you even think about controlling another person when you cannot yet control yourself? Aikido is not training to use violence against another. The standard in Aikido training is much higher than that. Because you are faced with this constant challenge, you don't need to seek enemies externally. Aikido training is like a question-and-answer session within yourself. Humbling yourself by bowing to the front of the *dojo* and to your partners directs your training toward (and against) yourself. That is why there are no tournaments in Aikido.

A Zen priest once told me, "Even a small stone thrown in a river sinks. However, with a big enough boat, you can carry even a big stone across the river." A stone sinks in water, regardless of size. But by using a boat, we can circumvent this fact.

The same is true of people. We are only human. We are not gods. But we can accomplish great things using outside forces and energies, which are to us as a boat is to a stone. What is important is to look at yourself, train yourself and improve yourself. You don't need to be better or stronger than anybody else; you only need to overcome yourself, control yourself so you don't become arrogant, humble yourself in *seiza* and *rei* so that you will see where you need to go. That is the training of Aikido, the training of your mind.   ~~~

Chapter 6

There Are Two Of You

Let's do some stretching exercises with legs outstretched. Don't look at the people around you, because they are not your reflections. They differ from you in age, occupation, physical condition, body type, and weight. These exercises are something you do for yourself. No matter how much someone else can stretch, it doesn't affect you. You must not compare yourself with others and feel either discouraged or smug about how you are doing.

Figure 6-1: The point isn't whether you do "better" or "worse" than others, but whether you do better than you have done before.

Keep your back straight and inhale, then bend toward your knees, keeping your back straight, while exhaling. It hurts a bit, doesn't it? Of course! This is a stretching exercise, and without a little bit of pain, you are not stretching!

In stretching exercises, you can see two parts of yourself. Stretch exercises are painful at first, but you don't need help from other people or from a machine to stretch, because the exercises are for yourself and you alone have to do them. Two of you are living in your body, just as two of me live in my body. Let's say one is the good and the other the bad. The bad in you might say, "This is it! I can't stretch any farther." Then let the good in you say, "Come on, do a little more. One more inch." The bad says, "This body is very stiff, and it's been this way for a long time." The good says, "Well, I already paid for this Aikido lesson. I've got to get something out of it." We might call the bad the "negative" mind, and the good the "positive" mind (Figure 6-2).

Of course, neither mind is always dominant in your life; everyone tends to move back and forth. Too positive a mind can become a very heavy burden on your shoulders. We all need to loosen up sometimes, though generally the more positive the mind, the more productive the life. What is important is to keep a positive mind as often as possible.

Figure 6-2: Let your positive mind triumph over your negative mind.

In stretching, the negative and positive fight over whether to quit or to stretch one more inch. It becomes not only a physical exercise, but also a way of training the mind. If this stretching were merely a physical exercise, you could have somebody push you from behind and become more flexible that way. But one of the most important aspects of this exercise is overcoming your own negative mind without outside help. This experience will eventually lead to a sense of confidence that you can exchange your negative mind for a positive one.

Without an element of mental training, any martial art has little effect on your daily life. In everyday life, whether your head can touch your knees or not doesn't make any difference, does it? Is your supervisor more limber than you? Are college professors required to be physically limber? Of course not. Having "limber" on your resume doesn't win very many jobs. These are irrelevant issues. In one sense, having a flexible body doesn't make you a better person (though you may be healthier). But the mind training that goes with it does.

Here is a visualization to use when stretching. Picture a traffic light with red, yellow and green signals. Many people follow the green light when doing stretch exercises. It means "no problem." Some stretch as far as the yellow signal, slowing down but trying hard. The red is, of course, too dangerous to try. In training, whatever it might be, it is essential that you reach into the zone of the yellow light frequently. When you do this, it should be voluntary and intentional. You shouldn't have anybody pushing from behind. Only you know when your "signal" turns red. Being aware of your limits is important so you can continuously give yourself new goals. You were much more flexible when you were a child than you are now. Realizing this helps you challenge yourself to regain what you once had. It works. You might not fully recover the flexibility of your childhood, but you will definitely improve.

Now you are headed in a positive direction! You must not dream of fighting another individual before you gain flexibility and control of your own body. It is like thinking of passing a marathon runner before you are able to run the distance. When a person tries to create a shape with clay, the clay must be soft. If the clay is hard, water must be added and it must be softened before a pot can be started. Similarly, you must "soften" your body in order to control it.

Many people come to my *dojo* expecting to learn a Japanese martial art instantly. They must first realize the purpose of the training, and at the same time see that the training will be a challenge to their own minds and bodies. The stretching exercises are the first step toward helping them realize these things.

Open your legs now. A little bit wider. Then bend your body forward with an exhalation. You may think you've bent as far as you can, but you can go a little further. Your negative mind tells you "that's it," but your positive mind can let you push down an inch more. Which mind you choose to listen to is your decision. You control it. You must overcome yourself before asking for somebody else's help. You can learn a lot about yourself and your mind from these simple stretching exercises. How far you can bend is not nearly as important as how much further you try to stretch.   ~~~

Chapter 7

Take Off Your Work Hat

In my *dojo*, the first 15 minutes of class are spent on stretches, warm-ups and Aikido exercises. The first day of the beginner's course is used to explain the stretching and Aikido exercises because these are such important parts of Aikido training. As mentioned, one purpose of stretching and warm-up exercises is to achieve a balance between body movements and breathing. The Aikido exercises explained in this chapter lead the student into the basic movements of Aikido techniques. You can practice these stimulation exercises outside of Aikido class as health exercises, and they will help stiff shoulders, headaches and other tension-related problems.

When I teach these stimulation exercises, beginners tend to be tense, muscles stiffened all over their bodies. I tell them to relax, but the shoulders remain raised and there is a line between the eyes. "Please take off your work hat. Your day's work is done and you don't need to bring it here. You cannot accomplish anything if you are tense." Breathe out deeply, yes, then inhale into the abdomen with the arms extended. Use this same breathing while doing your wrist exercises. Repeat this calm and smooth breathing, and you can get away from your work or irritating home issues. With tight shoulders, your frustration will only increase.

Nikkyo Exercise

The first exercise is a stimulation of the wrist (Figure 7-1). It serves as a warm-up for wrist immobilization techniques (*katamewaza*). Repeat the movement on the left wrist, twisting and releasing with each count (one, two, three, four and five). Then do the same on the right wrist. Repeat the process on each wrist several times.

In the science of *Shiatsu* (acupressure or finger massage), the line of stimulation or the line of effect of touching a specific part of the body is called the "keiraku". The *nikkyo* exercise follows the *keiraku* for *rokuzo (kanzo, shinzo, hizo, jinzo, haizo* and *shinpo)*. So this first stimulation exercise serves two purposes:

1. strengthening and stretching the wrists.

2. providing healthy stimulation of the circulatory system.

Kotegaeshi Exercise

The second stimulation exercise is a warm-up for techniques called *kotegaeshi*. In *Shiatsu* terms, stimulation from this exercise follows the *keiraku* for *roppu (tanno, shocho, daicho, boko, i* and *sansho*)(Figure 7-2).

To do *kotegaeshi*, put your left palm in front of your face. Grip the area below the thumb with the four fingers of your right hand, and pull away; at the same time, push between the last two knuckles of the left hand with your right thumb. As you feel the hand twist, lower the arm to navel-height, increasing the twisting for maximum stimulation.

Figure 7-1: The *nikkyo* wrist stimulation exercise.

Rowing Exercise

The following exercise is for extension and relaxation. It is called the rowing exercise. (Figure 7-3) The name comes from the technique of sculling a boat. It is best to live in a positive and extended way, but you cannot be doing so all day every day. You need to relax sometimes. The best balance is to extend and focus when you need to, and relax the rest of the time. This is more easily said than achieved!

You need to train yourself to extend, and, more importantly, to relax at will. You can accomplish this with the following simple exercises. Using your body to extend and relax stimulates or influences your mind to do the same.

The forward motion of the rowing exercise is similar to that used in pushing a stalled car out of an intersection: place your hands on the car, secure your feet in position, then push! Imagine doing just that, and think of your breathing. You exhale while pushing, and if you need to push some more, you stop and inhale before you push again.

The same is true in daily life. "Extending" in work or business is like pushing a car. You cannot do it all the time. You need to take a break, relax, so that new energy will generate. Most of us know that, but, strangely, it is very difficult to switch our minds easily, especially after extending for awhile. You think to yourself that you have to relax, yet it becomes harder and harder to do so. Heading home after a hard day's work, you must face crowds and traffic.

Figure 7-2: The *kotegaeshi* wrist stimulation exercise.

In Japan we use the expression, "no time to breathe" to indicate a very busy situation. This expression means that there is no time for calm, ordinary breathing. What do you have to do to return to ordinary breathing? First, exhale deeply. This brings relaxation naturally. When both body and mind are tense, the only thing that consciously leads to relaxation is controlled breathing. Add simple body movements to controlled breathing, and the effect doubles.

Habits are formed by repetition of an action, consciously or unconsciously. By practicing extension and relaxation exercises every day at the *dojo*, Aikidoists develop an ability to switch back and forth between extension and relaxation. Many Aikido students find that practice helps them relax when they want to.

To perform the rowing exercise, place your left foot about a shoulder's width ahead of your right foot and let your body face straight forward, not diagonally. Relax both arms. On the count of "one," draw your hands up next to the hips to navel height as you inhale. Then with an exhalation, extend both arms with wrists bent, palms down. With the "o" of "one", you begin raising your arms, with "n" your lungs are filled, and with "e" your arms extend forward. When "one" is completed, your front knee is bent and your body has moved forward to balance above this knee. It is like pushing a car. Here in the *dojo* you are not pushing a car, but instead everything that is in front of you. What? There is nothing? No, no, you are wrong. Your objectives, purposes and goals are in front of you. Anything imaginable is in front of you. And you are pushing it with all your might. Then on the count of "two" you return to the starting point by reversing the movement with a light inhalation. Your whole body relaxes. Forget everything you were pushing a moment ago. This has to be done with conscious effort. Even if you cannot relax your mind after a few times, your body is relaxing because of your breathing. Within twenty repetitions of this exercise your mind will follow your body and breathing. Do the exercise again, but with the right foot forward.

Let me give you a visual example so you can more clearly see the effect of this exercise. Imagine yourself standing alone on a beach, watching a wave move in from the distance. The wave grows higher and higher as it approaches the beach. Now superimpose your daily life over the image of the wave. The wave comes closer and gets very high, and at one point it reaches its apex. Then the wave crashes down on the sand and flows up the beach. You see many bubbles and the wave goes back into the sea. Well, watch out! The next wave is almost here. And the next one, and the next .... In your life too, there are many waves coming toward you, one after another and if you can relax between waves, you are in much better shape to handle the waves. Don't consider the waves as your enemies, because you cannot stop them. Don't try to fight the wave. Take them as friends, and enjoy them, ride them.

Figure 7-3: The rowing exercise is fluid and relaxed, yet powerful.

With "o" the wave gets higher, with "n" it reaches the peak and with "e" it crashes, then subsides with "two". Ideally, extension and relaxation training has the rhythm of surf on a beach.

When your imagination, body movement, and breathing don't match, the exercise is just a series of body movements. But when these three things match, you experience the true training of Aiki. Your mind is in harmony with your surroundings.   ~~~

Chapter 8

Open Your Hands

The open hand is emphasized in Aikido; making fists is not. Try doing a stretching exercise with your hands tightly fisted. Or try a breathing exercise with tight fists. In Aikido, most movements are done with open hands because it is more natural.

Two people are giving speeches. One is very energetically waving his fists. Another is making a point with his hands open and big flowing motions. Let's look at them a little closer. The former is likely to be attacking something, with a deep line between his eyes. The latter shows a calm expression, maybe even a smile. From the point of view of Aikido, fists indicate aggressiveness and narrow thoughts; open hands indicate peaceful and open thoughts (Figure 8-1).

Those who speak of *ki* say that it flows through open hands, but not through fists. Actually, open hands are natural in a calm and peaceful person. When you meet people, do you greet them with fists, or do you open your hands to shake? When you call your child to you, do you wave a fist or an open hand? Images and statues of religious leaders show open hands. This is also an Aikido pose.

Figure 8-1: An open hand is an expression of peace and harmony.

What do you want when you tense up your shoulders and make fists? You look like a baby wanting to have its diaper changed or wanting to be fed! If any discomfort or needs are making you tense, you must realize that the source is within you.

Some people are satisfied with two small meals a day, yet others are not satisfied until they have a big steak. Some people live peacefully under bridges or in alleys, yet others who live in penthouses complain that the elevator takes too long. The differences come from inside each person.

Now, loosen up your shoulders and open your hands. Relax and let your greed and desire fall out of your hands to the floor. Why do you need to open your hands to be calm? Is it only a pose? When the sea is rough, many whales could jump into the air, yet go unnoticed. But when the water is calm, a little fish can jump and is noticed. With a calm mind, you can see, hear and feel many things which you might not otherwise. You can then find proper and smooth actions to deal with them.

Figure 8-2: There is a natural explanation why your hands open wide in an emergency or moment of fright.

If you touch a hot pot accidentally, what will your reaction be? "Ouch!" and both hands open. If someone sneaks up on you from behind and surprises you, part of your immediate and unconscious reaction is to open your hands. *Shiatsu* theory says that opening the hands is a natural reaction to counter the sudden rise of blood pressure caused by the sense of emergency.

Ikkyo Undo

The next Aikido exercise is called *ikkyo undo*. It starts from the same position as the rowing exercise. On the count of "one," swing both hands out and up. The hands are open and the palms face out as if you were catching a basketball in front of your face. With the "o" of "one," you inhale, with "n," you begin raising the arms and exhaling, and with "e," you reach maximum extension and finish the exhalation. Hands are wide open. With the count "two," release and swing the arms back down to a relaxed position at your sides.

Figure 8-3: *Ikkyo Undo* - learning to extend.

When something happens to you suddenly, you react first by opening your hands. Even at the moment of danger, you need to remain as calm in your mind as possible. *Ikkyo undo* and the rowing exercise are practiced for extension and release at will. They help develop stability in sudden danger. In other words, these exercises allows you to take advantage of your natural reactions and improve on them. No one needs fists to properly react to unexpected danger.
~~~

Chapter 9

Things Have More Than One Side

In previous exercises, the "front" was set in one direction. But in real life, you don't have one front side. When necessary, you must turn in whatever direction your attention is needed. Thus, the direction you face becomes the front. In other words, you could say that there is no back side.

Zengo Undo

The next exercise, *zengo undo*, is a simplified practice of extension, using just two directions. First, perform *ikkyo undo* to the front (toward the *dojo's* shrine), then as soon as you relax, pivot to face the opposite end of the *dojo*. That side now becomes the "front," so extend fully as in *ikkyo undo* in that direction, then relax. Pivot back to the shrine again, and continue this exercise of extension in different directions.

Figure 9-1: *Zengo Undo* - learning to extend in various directions.

When you drive a car, you pay attention to what's ahead when moving forward. When you drive backward, you first have to shift to reverse, then check behind and move hands and feet to direct the car. You know what would happen if you backed up paying attention only to your front, or drove forward with all your attention on the rear view mirror!

In martial arts terms, you move to neutralize the attack of an opponent to your front. Then you must turn to face other attackers. Too much attention focused on one opponent leaves you unaware of others. You must learn to switch your attention quickly, or you will not survive.

Pay full attention to what you are facing here and now. When that is taken care of, release attention completely so you can face the next problem or project. *Ikkyo undo* to the front and back teaches change of position, situation, concentration and extension.

Tenkan Undo

Add footwork to the previous exercise and you have *tenkan undo*. This exercise requires very simple footwork, but it seems very difficult for most beginners. Start with one foot in front, as for *ikkyo undo*, then take a step forward with the rear foot.

Figure 9-2: *Tenkan Undo* - adding footwork to your extension exercises.

Pivot 180 degrees on that foot and bring the other foot behind you by taking a step back with it. Repeat the same footwork to return to your original position. There are only two steps for each turn!

When I explain the exercise as simply as this, beginners' steps become light and the exercise is carried out with ease. The previous exercise was done in the same spot and extended in two directions. This exercise is done with steps, adding another dimension to concentration training. On the count of "one," inhale, take a step forward and extend a hand. With exhalation, turn, step back and extend both arms, hands open and palm up, to your new front. On the count of "two," reverse direction in the same manner. This training develops the ability to deal with problems in a more active way. Of course, all movements have to be matched by breathing, so that no matter how fast you move you can maintain the calmness in your mind.

In martial terms, when an attacker moves in, you can use *tenkan* to turn your body to avoid the aggression while checking to see what is behind you. I will explain this element later in more detail.

I often add the following test to the *tenkan undo* exercise. In doing *tenkan undo*, I count "one," "two," "one," "two," with a regular cadence for a while, then suddenly stop the count. Some students keep on moving, and some stop. Those who keep going are doing the exercise merely as physical training, without mental training by listening to my count. Next, I tell students that I will strike them with my hand, and they are supposed to move to avoid this. At first, many of them move when I slide up a little or make an exaggerated inhalation. After doing this exercise for a while, they begin to make a better judgement of which of my actions imply a real attack and which are a bluff. It is very interesting to watch them develop this new sense.

I add seriousness to the exercise next. I pick up a *bokken* (wooden sword), swing it down with a "whoosh," and remind them that it would hurt ("itai," in Japanese) if it hit anyone. The movement is the same without the *bokken*. There is only a small change, and every student is at least ten feet away from me. The *bokken* is about three feet long, so the only way you could be hit is if it slipped out of my hands and flew at you, which is not likely. But the difference becomes great to the students. Some get very tense, some turn red from the tension, and some cannot even keep their balance. And this is all before I even make a move! What does this mean? It means that people easily lose their presence of mind when a threatening thing or action appears in front of them. In this case, it doesn't matter how far away I am. The student's mind decides that it will be painful if he is hit, thus the exercise is very dangerous and threatening. That fear makes him very nervous and tense.

In this exercise, then, you learn to find calmness and maintain it in very tense situations. This is a major objective in the practice of Aikido. A tense situation is created easily in the practice of martial arts, since many of us perceive these arts as fairly dangerous activities. As time goes on, and students become black belts, they are hardly affected by such tense situations any longer.

On the other hand, students must not begin to take their practice for granted. I see many students, especially visitors from other schools, doing their exercises mechanically. You need not do the exercise fast, but pay attention to all that you are doing and everything around you. Like a butterfly flying casually among flowers, checking out the interesting ones, we can learn to deal with things that are happening here and there with calm attention to each one. That is *tenkan undo*.

Iriminage Undo

The next exercise is very similar to *tenkan undo*. In fact, it uses the same footwork. The difference is in the hand movement. This exercise is called iriminage undo. The hands move up and down, perpendicular to the floor. You begin this exercise with the left foot forward and both hands down on our right side. With the first step, both hands are raised above your head, and with the step back, they are brought back down, but to the left side of your body. The right foot is now in front.

Figure 9-3: *Iriminage Undo* - a high, sweeping motion with the hands as you turn.

Compare this to *tenkan undo*, where the hands are kept at about the same height at all times, moving parallel to the floor. Iriminage undo moves vertically, relating to your emotional ups and downs. It gives an energetic impression. In other words, *tenkan undo* is like turning around holding a can full of paint in your hands, so to speak, and *iriminage undo* is like turning around with a large brush with plenty of paint on it, brushing it on a wall, and becoming calm after each stroke.

On the count of "one," inhale, raise both arms, step forward, and begin to turn. Continue to step back while bringing the hands down and exhaling. Now you are facing the opposite direction. On the count of "two," reverse your actions, movements matching breathing. Repeat this several times. With this exercise, you again practice changing the direction of concentration, with a greater level of energy than in *tenkan undo*. Energy is raised with your upward arm motion and returns to a calm attentive stance at the end of each turn.

I mentioned earlier that no one can remain extended all the time. Those who try to will eventually break down. We all need to control our extension level in daily life. *Iriminage undo* guides us to relax at the end of each period of extension.

Of course, there are Aikido techniques which can be applied when facing a physical attack, and I will explain this further in later chapters. But Aikido exercises relate in a very practical way to our real life needs. In work and in family life we must attend with full concentration. No one works wanting to be fired. No one tries to break up his or her family. We do our best to maintain and improve life. But when we rest, we should rest fully.

There are many more Aikido exercises, but these are enough to start. An important thing is to fully realize the fact that all the exercises are done with commands from your mind. Of course, the ideal is to have positive, clear, and energetic signals from your mind when doing exercises. Matching your movements and breathing helps generate these ideal signals. When the physical and psychological elements of an exercise are harmonized, your strength and energy are amplified several times. ~~~

Chapter 10

It Is Natural To Fall

One more type of exercise is essential in Aikido training. It is necessary to take falls as a part of Aikido, so it is in your best interest to know how to fall safely and smoothly. As the conclusion to this section on Aikido exercises, I would like to describe how to learn *ukemi*.

There are no tournaments in Aikido. Therefore, we don't have to worry about being thrown. However, we do fall. I'm certain that you are puzzled by this contradiction. Let me clarify this point.

There are two ways to fall: against your will, as when being thrown by an opponent, or at your will, as in the case of protecting yourself or regaining an advantageous position. In Aikido, the latter type of fall is practiced. If you have seen an Aikido demonstration, you have noticed that one person in each demonstration takes falls (flying or rolling). When I do demonstrations for schools and other organizations, the audience often asks why my partner always loses. I try to explain to them that falling doesn't mean defeat, but their strong association of falling with defeat cannot easily be altered.

Figure 10-1: Falling doesn't mean defeat. Let yourself go!

Please don't misunderstand this. In Aikido, the person falling is not being thrown against his will, but is taking falls with clear, positive intention. The falls are not being "done to" them; they are actively "doing" the falls for themselves.

Figure 10-2: Who is really in charge of your falls? You are.

In sports like boxing and judo, falling means defeat, so competitors do their best to avoid falling. In competitions, falling indicates a bad result. In Aikido, on the contrary, falling is done to protect yourself. There is no concept in Aikido of winning or losing against others, so falling doesn't have such negative connotations. When you trip on a stone or slip on ice and lose your balance, you don't think about defeating the stone or ice. You think about not hurting yourself. Similarly, in Aikido, falling means avoiding momentary danger and moving to a safer position with regained ground. In this regard, *ukemi* by itself is a very important and useful technique in Aikido.

Now let us start the actual practice of falls. First, sit with your legs in front, almost like sitting "Indian style," but with one leg somewhat extended. Straighten your back as you inhale, and roll back while exhaling with the count "one." Then roll back up while inhaling with my count "two". Pull your chin in (or try to look at your navel) so you will be sure not to hit your head. Repeat this several times. This is a warm up for rolling back from a standing position, but don't think of it as merely a physical exercise. Throughout the previous exercises a clear separation of extension and relaxation was emphasized. The same is true for this exercise. The sitting position is calm. Rolling back and coming up is active. Then you go back to the calm upright sitting position. This matching of movement and mind is an important aspect of the exercise.

Figure 10-3: Sit calmly at both "ends" of a sitting back roll.

Imagine that you are reading a book. Suddenly your child starts crying in the bedroom. You have to put down your book and go to the room to attend to the child. Soon after, the child goes back to sleep and you return to your reading. Then someone rings the doorbell and you have to get up to answer. The phone rings, or the washing machine buzzes; it is a busy day, and it is difficult to find time to concentrate on reading.

Figure 10-4: Doing a back roll from the standing position requires a little more energy, the way a car requires more gas when going uphill.

Put yourself in this type of situation when you practice back rolls. Move and stop with full awareness. This is a very simple exercise, but repetition is very important. Keep in mind that "stop" doesn't mean "dead." It is like the idling of a car engine, which is different from shutting off the engine. In idle, the tachometer does not read 0 RPMs. Zero means the car is off, which is a completely different state. Keep yourself in idle, and whenever necessary give more gasoline to work the engine harder, then return to idle when the work is done. If you keep your gas pedal to the floor from morning to night, even a Japanese car will fall apart soon! It is important to return to calm (idle) quickly, as well as to generate maximum energy quickly when it's time to move.

After practicing the back roll exercise from a sitting position comes the back roll from a standing position. Imagine that you are driving on a highway. You see a hill ahead. When you have acknowledged it, you will shift gears and step on the gas. Nearing the top of the hill, you must decide when to shift back and release the gas to a cruising level.

Back rolls from a standing position are almost like driving on a highway with many hills. It requires a little bit more energy to stand up than to come back to the sitting position. You must also intend to stand up. Nobody can stand up while thinking "do not stand up" or "fall back." You have to want to stand up mentally before it is physically possible. You have to extend more energy to your body, and once you stand up, work harder to return your energy level to a calm state. Of course this is an important technique for protecting yourself when you fall backward, but more importantly, it is training in changing your awareness.

The back roll exercise is also a health treatment. When you roll back, your body is pressed against the mat, thus stimulating *Shiatsu* (acupressure) points located on your back. Also in this exercise your stomach muscles are tightened and relaxed, which stimulates your digestive system. These are additional benefits of the back roll exercise.

Forward rolls are used to protect yourself when you fall forward. The forward roll is similar to rolling a big hoop. The concept of this roll is to avoid concentrating on one spot (such as the head, neck, or hand) the impact of falling forward. This is done by shifting your weight smoothly across many contact points with the ground. The forward roll is also a good health treatment as well as clear expression of personality and attitude.

At NIPPON KAN, a children's Aikido class is held three times a week. The children are very active and as soon as they change into their workout uniforms and step onto the mat, they start running around and rolling. Occasionally, we have a brand new student. At first, the new student just watches the other students, but soon she joins the rest in running around before class begins. When it comes to rolling, she hesitatingly tries to copy, thinking "Everybody else is doing it, so I can, too."

If we put all beginners together in one room and instructed them in doing rolls, they probably would not learn as quickly as they do among other, more advanced students. When an instructor explains how to do rolls, the children think it is a special kind of movement. That adds a complication in their minds and makes the next step very difficult. In addition, there may be pressure from the instructor or parents in the child's mind: "I must do as told," (a very obedient idea); or, "I must do as told, or my dad will be mad," (an intimidated idea); or "I must do as told, or I don't get a toy," (a very calculating idea). What's been taught in their homes becomes apparent in their practice attitudes.

I brought up the example of children's class because the same is true in adult classes. Let's look at your present condition. Can you run and roll around freely like a child? Until when were you able to do that? Try to remember. Of course, the answer varies from one individual to another. If you were involved in sports in high school or college, you were running and rolling around until then. But if you spent most of high school and college in libraries or labs, then you stopped such activities earlier. If you were born in a city and have no brothers or sisters, then your condition is different from individuals who were born and raised on farms with lots of children nearby.

Regardless of your background, once you got out of school and started working, you probably didn't have many opportunities for running and rolling around. In the city, it is as though people are living in body casts. A person doesn't have a chance to fall at all in the city. As recreation, some people play ball games, ski, skate, jog or bowl, but in any event, falling is considered a mistake. At work, most people have to dress up. You must face work with a straight back and try to walk gracefully. Fashion magazines are filled with images of elegant poses. Health clubs are filled with people who wish to gain the right physique to match fashionable ideals. None of these people is thinking of falling down, even safely and gracefully.

In this society, falling has a very negative impression. Falling down is associated with defeat or mistakes. It doesn't look good. If you are unfortunate enough to fall, you try to regain the upright position as soon as possible. If I fall on a crowded street, I will get up quickly and keep walking as if nothing has happened - and then find a place where nobody is watching to rub where it hurts.

In an adult beginners' class, when I say for the first time, "Now we will practice forward rolls - follow my assistants," no one follows the smooth rolls the assistants demonstrate. If I explain how to roll step by step, new students still don't want to move. In this situation, students always compare themselves with others. "Can I do it like that?" or "Can I roll as well as the other beginners?" or "I don't want to look bad." In our society we are conditioned to view ourselves from a certain angle, and often that view inhibits us. We are no longer as innocent as children, so it is hard for us to learn something new. Generally speaking, children don't feel as much pressure as adults do in this kind of situation; they enjoy trying new things. If you could only be like a child, it would be a lot easier to learn this!

Figure 10-5: Don't worry about looking bad. Just try it!

Therefore, when first starting forward rolls, I simply tell the beginning students to go ahead and roll, and assure them that it doesn't matter at all how they do it. The most terrible roll is still much better than doing nothing. It doesn't matter if you look good doing a forward roll now or not, because if you keep practicing, you will look good soon. Once the initial fear of not hurting or embarrassing yourself is dispelled, practice becomes much smoother.

The practice of falling is indeed a personal challenge for yourself. You must learn to be open in front of fellow students. Women with fine makeup, fashionable warm-up wear and nice perfume, as well as athletic-looking men tend to have trouble with this hang-up. They want to achieve perfection from the beginning and demand complete, detailed instruction before even trying. Once the procedure is explained to them, they concentrate too much on doing it right so they can look good. They become tense and uncoordinated under these circumstances - or I should say their uncoordination is emphasized. After a round of this, they look at me as if to imply that I didn't give them proper instruction. I look back at them and say, "Roll around like an innocent kid!" You're not used to rolling so it's O.K. to look bad while learning this. Don't compare yourself with others, just do your best at not hurting yourself. Then your front rolls will improve quickly.

At the Aikido *dojo* you can enjoy falling and learning to roll gracefully. This adds an additional dimension to your daily life, and can positively affect your personality as well. Many beginning students find that learning such activities as rolling forward and backward are actually pleasant experiences. Of course you may feel sore at first, or dizzy, but if you compare doing this for the first time with falling on a concrete surface by accident, practicing on the mat is much easier and safer.

The practice of rolling brings out your original instinct for protecting your body when you fall. You should be aware that you have, until now, forgotten this important skill. ~~~

Figure 10-6: After awhile, rolling becomes easy, and begins to feel good.

Chapter 11

Your Partner Is Not Your Enemy

At NIPPON KAN, the first two beginner sessions are spent on the stretch, warm-up and Aikido exercises. This is because I would like beginning students to understand the important relationships of mind, breathing and body movements. Some students obviously feel that they are not here to learn these relationships but to learn martial art techniques. Some of them clearly display dissatisfaction or boredom by yawning or leaning back on their hands. This type of student tends to drop out of the course soon.

There is yet another purpose in the extensive emphasis on the exercises. I avoid getting into the techniques of Aikido at the start so that I can undo some of the preconceptions and prejudices that new students bring to the *dojo*.

The information most beginning students have is what's available through TV programs, movies and magazines. Before starting the practice of actual techniques, I like to allow enough time for students to lose their preconceptions of the martial arts, to become aware of the stiffness of their own bodies, and also to realize how easy it is to lose their balance. Before thinking about taking someone else's balance, students should learn to maintain their own. Students must prepare their minds and bodies to be able to practice a martial art.

When working on clay for pottery, a person must knead the clay to make it soft, then get used to the feel of the clay under her hands. With this accomplished, she can finally start working on shaping the clay. Without this preparation, a pot may crack or explode in the kiln. It is the same for martial arts practice. If you start rigorous martial arts training without knowing your body's limits, you will hurt yourself.

Eventually, though, practice with a partner begins. As I have mentioned, there are no tournaments in Aikido. Therefore, the person in front of you is not your enemy or opponent, but a situation to be dealt with. Imagine yourself in an office. You get a big rush job in. You don't have time to take a break or to eat. The phone keeps ringing. But this doesn't change you. You are you, and if you don't like the situation, you can quit. If you don't want to quit, then you have to deal with the situation. In many cases, we unnecessarily make these situations our enemies.

In Aikido practice, your partner is a fellow human being. He or she is an individual who has a different background, different physical ability, and perhaps a different motive for starting Aikido practice. You two might have some similarities, but you are basically different people. To make this different individual move in a way that you want him or her to is not an easy task. It is much easier to work on a sandbag or a barbell. Your partner, however, is not a dummy (more on this in Chapter 14).

After demonstrating what movement the students should work on, I tell them to find partners and start practicing. Interestingly, at first the students look around but don't move. After awhile, couples who came to the *dojo* together pair up. Pairs of friends follow. Finally the rest of the students pair up to start practice. In pairing up for practice, two different individuals are involved. It is a fairly complicated process because it is not a decision of a single mind. Why do they hesitate? Of course at first, the students who came by themselves don't know if the others came together. It is self-consciousness and caution among strangers. Thoughts like "What if I'm rejected?" or "This guy looks tough" prevent them from pairing up quickly. When two people know each other, there are fewer obstacles. Seeing the others pair up makes the rest feel easier about finding partners. When the slowest group finally makes pairs, they tend to be man and man, or woman and woman. This is interesting, too.

Within a few weeks, the students begin to pair up quickly, but there are still slow movers. Quiet individuals tend to wait for others to come to them, and if there is an odd number of students, one of them gets left out. Sometimes, I raise my voice, saying, "Quickly, find a partner!" Once they get over their shyness, they do all right.

Just from watching students find partners, you can see many different and interesting personalities. There is one type of person who is almost annoying. He or she makes easy judgments of others, and becomes selective in choosing partners. This person cannot find partners quickly because it takes time to choose just the "right" one. Other students won't move until somebody comes to them, believing all they have to do is wait and others will come to them. Fairly common is the person who, finding him-or herself without a partner, makes a trip to the restroom or changing room to make the point that he or she can do without the others. I've seen many people in this category, and all of them drop out before completing the course. One cannot practice Aikido without a certain amount of openness to new people as well as new ideas.

In my classes I instruct students to change partners frequently. In this way you can learn to practice with many different types of individuals, and avoid making harsh judgments about other students. When everyone can work with everyone else in the class, the class runs very smoothly. If you are thinking, "Oh, no. I don't want to work with this guy," you cannot really practice Aikido. There are different types of people: tall and short, big and small, stiff and soft, strong and weak, sweaty and perfumed. After all, we are all different and you should be able to work with different partners. If you are unwilling, it shows in your actions and your partner will be aware of it, making smooth practice difficult. Remember, your mind moves your body, and your body expresses your mind. You will be amazed at how much better you know a person after practicing together for five or ten minutes, with very few words spoken.

I often use the example of a whetstone and a knife. Your partner is your whetstone, and you are your partner's whetstone. In Aikido, you take turns throwing and falling, being the knife and the whetstone. This way, you can learn both techniques and falls. Whether you make your partner your enemy or friend is up to you.

Figure 11-1: An Aikido partnership is like a whetstone and knife. Respect your partners.

By about the fourth or fifth week, the beginning students become very proficient at working with different partners, because they have gotten over the initial mental block against the others and have learned something new about the variations of body types and personalities. Of course, the students do not realize this, and it is the instructor's job to point it out. This realization can turn into self-confidence - gained from the practice of Aikido!

Beginning students show their inner feelings in interesting ways. Here's an example: the *dojo* at NIPPON KAN is about 50 feet square. The south side is the front, where the shrine is. The entrance is located at the northwest corner. The mat is big enough for about 20 pairs of students to practice at one time. In early sessions of the beginner's course, new students tend to concentrate near the entrance, causing a space crisis in the room. I probably don't have to explain why this happens. At the beginning of the course the students are extremely cautious because of their preconceptions about martial arts. They are not really sure about what happens at a martial arts school. That uncertain feeling consciously or unconsciously makes them position themselves at the safest location - close to the exit. I often wonder if this is a souvenir that Bruce Lee left in the mind of the American public. However, as students get used to the *dojo* and to Aikido, they begin to spread out more evenly on the mat.

In this chapter I have pointed out how behavior is influenced by changes in your mind, which are often governed by preconceptions. In dealing with other individuals you should remember that they are governed by the same conditions. In a beginners' class, nobody is thinking about overcoming or overpowering fellow students. Students come here with basically harmonious spirits. If this harmonious spirit is expressed in action, a whetstone - a friend - is gained; if not, an enemy is created. If you think your partner is your enemy, then your partner will think of you as an enemy. Instead, think of your partner as a mirror which lets you see yourself. Practice as if you are cleaning a mirror. The cleaner your mirror becomes, the clearer the image of yourself. Cooperation is an important attitude in practicing with partners. After all, you are borrowing your partner's body to improve yourself.~~~

Figure 11-2: Fear of the unknown keeps new students near the door for the first few sessions!

Chapter 12

Your Partner Is A Mosquito

By the title of this chapter, I don't mean to encourage you to take your partner lightly! Please read on.

Earlier in the book, there is an explanation of *tenkan undo*, the 180 degree step-and-turn movement. From this exercise you can gain an important insight, especially when seeing it practiced by children.

First, the children are taught the steps involved in *tenkan undo* and they practice the exercise for a while. Then I take out a plastic toy sword, which was given to me by a student as a joke. "Now, I will try to hit you with this sword. You must get away so you don't get hit. Use the steps you just learned," I tell them. I hold the sword in front of me and look at the children.

Some of them are already tense, some remain relaxed. Those over eight years old tend to be tense, but the younger ones tend to stay calm. What makes the difference? Think about it: the younger children don't have a clear idea of what it would be like to be hit by the plastic sword, or else they know that it really wouldn't hurt. So they don't worry about being hit, and instead take the exercise as a fun game. On the other hand, the older students have ideas about a situation in which an attack is imminent. The psychological pressure makes them tense.

When I switch the plastic sword for a wooden one, older students become even more tense, but the younger ones don't. Then I add more information. I hit my head lightly with the wooden sword, which makes a sound. I say, "Ouch!" I repeat this a couple of times so the children can relate the physical contact and pain. Then I conduct the same *tenkan undo* exercise. This time, all the children become somewhat tense, even the very little ones.

What can you learn from this lesson? You have already lived long enough to know how to gather information, process it, and act accordingly. When students first start practicing with partners, a kind of data processing takes place and controls behavior. The given (and assumed) information in this case is: this is a martial arts class; we are learning a technique to throw an attacker; the attacker is an enemy; the attacker is big; he seems to be a quick learner. And so on. This data processing takes place within you, and you create a situation of being controlled by your own fears. Even a master of martial arts cannot damage you without physical contact, yet you are tense with the mere thought of what's supposed to occur with your partner.

You might be able to relate to the following examples. You study very hard for an important exam, worrying about what kinds of questions will be asked. You make sure that you are ready for any question, but on the exam day when you enter the testing room, everybody else seems much better prepared than you. Then you find you can't answer the questions to your satisfaction.

Or, you prepare a speech to give in front of hundreds of people, and you memorize every line perfectly. But when you get on the stage and look at the audience, you forget your lines.

Or, you have an interview with a major corporation, and you believe you are well qualified. But when you see the huge building and luxurious offices, you become intimidated and can't present yourself well. I can think of many examples like these. The exam won't bite you. The audience won't throw rocks at you. The building won't crush you. You fear them because the fear is within you. You are making these situations intimidating.

The very first technique practiced at NIPPON KAN starts from a "hold-up" position. "Both hands in the air, and don't move." If you saw a knife or gun, you would do as told, wouldn't you? Partners stand face to face, and the "attacker" points an index finger at the defender's eye. The defender holds both arms up in the air.

When you raise both hands, you inhale. This is your energy building up within you. Your advantage is that your partner finished exhaling when she pointed her knife at you. As your energy gushes out with an exhalation, you quickly lower your hand on top of your partner's knife hand. By the time your partner catches your action and brings her energy level up (by inhaling) to react to your action, you are already in control of her hand.

This exercise illustrates the relationship between breathing and the build-up and release of energy. Inhalation is the charging of energy; exhalation is an explosion of energy. Nobody can poke accurately with a knife while inhaling.

Beginners cannot do this move smoothly, yet advanced students can easily do this type of exercise with real knives. The difference is in the preconception, or the data processing. Beginning students tend to concentrate only on grabbing the partner's hand. Yet the attacker doesn't really intend to poke your eyeball - he is doing this as practice. He doesn't have anything against you. But you try to grab his hand as if he were your real enemy. You repeat this over and over, and your partner does the same. After a while, I step in. "Hold on just a moment. I told you that this practice is to find out how smoothly and quickly you can move if you match your breathing and motion and maintain your balance. This is not practice in taking away weapons from a real attacker on the street. There is nothing to get too serious about. With a tense and overly serious attitude you can cause many problems in your daily lives." Women tend to understand the objective of this exercise more easily than men because most don't think in terms of overpowering the attacker. Men, on the other hand (especially tough-looking ones), have a harder time accepting this idea, because they try too hard to remove the threat by force. It is a *macho* attitude.

The "knife" (or finger) in front of you is like a mosquito flying around your face. You don't need to pull out a gun and shoot it down! Overkill is not necessary. It is good practice to learn to make your own move without being overly affected by what is in front of you. To strike down a knife is one of the simple lessons of Aikido, but from it we can learn the depth and wide application of martial arts training to daily life.   ~~~

Chapter 13

Learning From A Leaky Ceiling

During a busy lunch hour at a local hamburger stand, the melting snow on the roof was dripping through the leaky ceiling. There was a bucket and a sign: "Caution! Slippery!" I noticed two types of individuals pass the bucket while I was casually observing. One type looked at the sign and carefully walked around the bucket. Another type stopped for a moment and looked up to see what was going on. Both types checked the immediate problem - but one checked further into the source of the problem.

A person is holding you at knife point. You acknowledge the immediate problem. But if you place all of your attention on the knife, you won't be able to assess why you are in the situation, what the attacker has in his other hand, and what else is coming at you. Of course, you have to deal with the immediate danger, but at the same time, you need to know more about the situation surrounding you. So as you grasp the attacker's hand, you move back-to-back to him, to face the same direction the attacker is facing, and check the area that was just behind you. The steps are the same as *tenkan undo*. This way you can better position yourself against further complications. This is not only like checking the sign and bucket, but also for the root cause of the problem.

In a strict martial arts sense, this move is used to hold the attacker from the front and at the same time prepare against attacks from elsewhere, especially from behind. However, if I emphasize this point only, the class becomes a lesson in fighting skills. I believe it is a duty of instructors of traditional Japanese martial arts to arrange training so that it becomes applicable in a practical way to modern society. Instructors must provide clear explanations of how Aikido principles apply to today's living.

For example, let's assume that you are walking on a sidewalk downtown. A child is riding a bicycle toward you. You note the problem and think of possible actions to take. What would you do? Stay there and collide with the child? Push him away so he won't collide with you? Jump aside to avoid collision? Think of the possible results of your actions. You know what will happen if you stay there. If you push the child away, he might be injured, though you might come out unharmed. It seems that jumping away is the preferable action. But where? If you jump into traffic, you might be hit by a car, a worse outcome than having a collision with a bicycle. The point is that it is dangerous to become overly involved or concerned only with the immediate problem you face. Aikido movements integrate general awareness of your surroundings with physical action.

I would like to share a few more examples. On a street, a person comes up to you to ask directions. You pay too much attention in giving the directions, and don't notice someone else sneaking up behind you. Or, you are working in the backyard and someone rings the front doorbell. You go inside the house to answer the door, forgetting to lock the back door behind you. While you are talking to the person at the front door, others come in from the back and steal your belongings. Yet another example is a rival company doing a sales campaign in a town your company needs in order to maintain market share. If your attention is too concentrated on that one rival company, you might overlook what other rivals are doing, resulting in a loss of market share to those other competitors. In another example, children are playing catch, and a child misses the ball. He chases after it into the street, not paying attention to oncoming cars. You see the child run out in front of your car and slam on the brakes, causing your car to spin into the other lane and hit a car coming from the opposite direction. We hear many similar stories every day.

Therefore, in this *tenkan* exercise, you practice avoiding the initial offensive while learning to position yourself to be able to check what else is happening around you. After checking the situation, you can come back to take care of the initial problem; proper movement has already positioned you for that as well.

At first, you practice this technique from a static position, facing the attacker's drawn knife. This simplifies the practice step. In reality, - things get a little more tricky. Nobody walks around holding a knife or gun in plain sight. (If they did, crime would be much easier to control!) Nobody walks around with his hands up in the air, either. People carry weapons in their pockets or bags so the rest of us don't see them. And weapons are not the only things that we hide. Although most people appear to be gentlemen and ladies (most of the time), they hide a potentially vicious nature within themselves. We all have this nature. (Figure 13-1)

When attending a business meeting, you carry your information in your briefcase, and your counterpart from the other company carries her information in her briefcase. You can never assess for sure what is in her briefcase. She can guess what is in your briefcase, but she is not sure either. You don't really know what her offer is until she shows you, and she doesn't know what you can offer until you show her.

If you had to live your life with your hands up all the time just because somebody might attack you, you would need more than one body to keep up with so much stress. You need to learn to pay attention when necessary - and as intently as necessary. So the next step in our practice is to begin the attack from a more natural position.

From a posture with both hands by his sides, the attacker raises a hand above his head and swings it down at you. It is very close to the action of drawing a gun from a holster and taking aim. We call this attack *shomenuchi*.

Figure 13-1: Everyone has different sides to their personalities.

Now let's look at the components of this attack. Although the action is completed when contact is made, it begins while the attacker's hands are still down in a natural position. With the beginning of his inhalation, the action begins. This is the "H" of "H-I-T." Finishing the inhalation while the hand moves up, is "I". And finally, the downswing of the hand (with an exhalation until contact) is "T". Actions before "H" are normal and natural, so you cannot be quite sure when the attack will take place. Of course, in a practice situation, you know at least that your partner will attack you. Then, what will be your defensive move?

You are driving on a two-way highway, and you spot a car at a distance coming toward you. It is a two-way highway, so you think nothing more of the car. Soon, you realize that the car is not moving in a straight line. It is swerving in and out of its lane, as though the driver is drunk. You become cautious and watch the car closely. You give as much space as possible to the drunken driver to avoid a collision. But when do you turn the steering wheel? If you do it after "H-I-T" - a collision - it is too late. When you start turning earlier, you have a better chance of avoiding the collision.

When your partner inhales to begin his attack, you should also inhale. When he starts to swing his hand down with an exhalation, you also exhale and turn next to him. This *tenkan*, or 180 degree turn, not only gets you out of danger, but also gives you a chance to scan what was behind you. You have also positioned yourself to grab the attacker's hand so you can then twist his wrist toward him, causing him to fall. This is a technique called *shomenuchi kotegaeshi*. With these maneuvers, you can check your surroundings as you deal with the front attack. Your surroundings include what is behind you, how many more attackers there are, what the terrain is like, where the sun is, and so on. With all this information perceived, you can select the safest or the most advantageous position for your next move, while using the initial attacker's body as your defensive shield against other attackers.

"Now that you know what to practice, go ahead and work out with your partner," I say, letting the students practice for a while, waiting for the right time to point out the next problem. ~~~

Chapter 14

Your Partner Is Not A Dummy

Have you ever seen a cat play with a stuffed mouse? It is just a cat playing with her toy, but you must have noticed that cats can get really rough sometimes. Similar scenes can be seen in an Aikido class, too.

Cats do not live by moral or common sense as humans do. Cats live by their instincts - or should I say a different set of morals than humans. Playing with a dummy mouse, to a cat, is a game of instinct. The cat holds the toy in her mouth, chews on it, scratches it, swings it around, throws it against walls, and so on.

A cat that was purring on your lap senses something and suddenly jumps down and runs away. A dog you are walking suddenly begins growling as he sees another dog. These are examples of animal instincts, and humans do similar things.

At first, lining up in the *dojo* and doing exercises, all new students are gentlemen and ladies. But as soon as they begin practicing techniques with partners, some of them turn into animals.

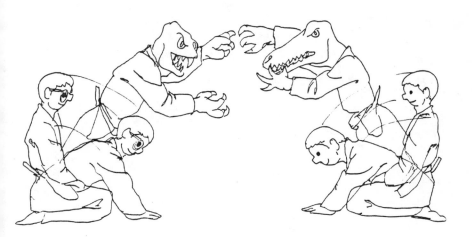

Figure 14-1: Why do some students turn into monsters when they begin working with a partner?

Your partner strikes at you. You grab his hand as if trying to catch a frisbee. Then you swing the hand which you just caught with all your might and all your attention. You don't care about your steps and movements. The only thing you are thinking about is throwing the attacker down. I say, "Remember that this exercise is only practice; the sequence is prearranged. Both partners understand what happens when: who attacks, who defends, who throws, who falls." It doesn't seem to have any effect. Then I try another approach. "Please think of how awkward you look," and I show them how they are doing, with some exaggeration. I show smooth and correct moves, too, so the students have visual guidance in practicing the technique.

To a beginning student, learning the first technique should be like learning to drive for the first time or learning to write the alphabet by tracing over letters. But at Aikido class, his mind is suddenly way ahead, picturing himself as the hero of a martial arts movie.

Figure 14-2: Knowing one technique doesn't make anyone an expert.

I can understand why many people act like this in class. In modern society, everyone is surrounded by constant pressure. A traffic accident, an accident at work, a robbery, a shooting or violent assault may befall you if you are not careful. Under these conditions you have learned to react strongly against whatever is coming at you, to protect yourself. No one can easily get away from this idea. It takes time to get used to Aikido training, which resembles a rehearsal for a play or for the action scene of a movie.

Let's again look at the example of children. A child's belt gets loose, and he goes back to his mother and asks her to fix it. She says, "No, do it yourself," and watches him try. When he successfully ties the belt, she gives him a hug. If a child is used to this pattern, he knows that if he does things right, he will be rewarded. So naturally, he tries to do things well. Children with very strict parents tend to overreact in this same type of practice. Or they shrink back when their partners raise their hands to hit. This is probably also an indication of family life. Some children pretend kicks or punches after a technique has been executed. This indicates that they have been influenced by martial arts movies and other violent media.

Defending yourself may be a very important part of human relations. Sadly, this defensive attitude can result in a personality which attempts to protect itself from everything else. If the defense falls, it's all over. Failure. Therefore anything coming from the outside world must be soundly defeated.

This phenomenon of actually trying to defeat the partner takes place in every beginners' class, as soon as we begin working on techniques. When I see this happening, my job as instructor is to make the students realize what they are doing. "Hold it! Wait a minute. Let's line up." They think, "Now what?"

I say, "What are you doing? I don't care how hard you twist your partner's hand and throw him down, but remember that your turn to be thrown will come next. Do you still want to throw your partner hard? You know what a Teddy bear is. You can pull its arms, punch it or throw it around, and it doesn't say a word. But your partner is not the same. Your partner is not a dummy." Then I show what they are doing with exaggeration. They laugh, and learn from their laughter. Some of them find their mimicked actions funny, then correct themselves. Others also see my performance as funny - but somehow fail to relate it to their own actions, and cannot learn the correct way.

In practice with partners, most students come to see how easily they can lose their calm rationality when faced with a problem. They realize that narrowly concentrated attention causes certain behavior patterns in class. By learning to turn their bodies when attacked, they find that they have options open to them, just as Aikido opens additional dimensions to their minds.

Some children cherish their teddy bears and take good care of them. Others poke pencils in them or tear their ears off. Your personality shows in the way you relate to your partners.

~~~

Chapter 15

Artists Don't Start With The Eyes

Let's say you are learning to swim and your first goal is to swim 25 meters. If you stop at 15 meters, then you haven't reached your goal. Aikido practice is the same. The first goal is to learn a few techniques. There is a starting point and an end point. If you don't get to the end point, you haven't accomplished the goal. For an attacker, raising the hand to strike is the starting point; the finish is the fall to the mat. For the defender, getting away from the attack, grabbing the attacker's hand, and twisting the wrist inward are the full "25 meters".

There are students who start toward the goal but never finish. The attacker strikes, and the defender moves out. But he doesn't like his position, so he asks the attacker to begin again. The attacker strikes again, and the defender moves and turns. This time he doesn't like where his hand ended up. So they try again. Again. And again. They will never reach the goal at this rate. I know they want to do it right, because if they don't, they won't look good. People with a strong sense of pride tend to go through this more often. Pride is a tricky thing, and sometimes it makes people immovable. People with jobs that require precision tend to have this problem. Those people who work using their creative senses, such as architects and artists, don't have much trouble here because they don't get hung up over finding the right answer.

For students who have trouble reaching the goal, I assist by leading the movements. I attack them and lead them in a way they can follow through the whole movement, which ends when I fall. Their bodies follow my movements, and their minds can "feel" the complete movement, thus reducing hesitation. In many cases, I hum while leading them around. Doing this reduces their tension, allowing the relaxed mind and body to move much more smoothly.

When you draw a picture, you first think of what is to be included, then draw an outline. In drawing a face, you start with an outline of the face, then decide where eyes, nose and mouth go. Nobody finishes a detailed eye first, then moves on to another part of the face. Similarly, when practicing a technique, you first have to learn the general flow of it. You shouldn't be concerned with details. Go through the whole motion with your body first; minor corrections can come later. This analogy helps students grasp their immediate goals. Then I add, "A master tightrope walker or a champion figure skater looked terrible when first starting. The advanced students sitting next to you were terrible when they started; I couldn't help laughing!" The new students begin to feel easy about "looking bad."

In practicing a technique, the minds of the students work first to move their bodies. As an instructor, I need to pay close attention and not put on too much pressure. I need to present each technique so that it looks very simple to their minds. Sometimes I sing a song while moving, and sometimes I imitate dance steps. There may be a method to explain movements using an indescribable and mysterious force such as *ki*. But I prefer to have the students realize that their minds are controlling their actions, and their minds are causing them to behave in various ways. Once they alter the perspective of their minds they smooth out their actions.

It is not as important to get the details right as it is to go through the whole movement repeatedly. If you go in the wrong direction occasionally, it's O.K. You can then go in the other direction and be on the right track. You don't need to punish yourself for little mistakes that you make in class.

A mind belongs to a person, and nobody else can do anything with it. The body is a faithful instrument which expresses the mind. You can become aware that when your body moves in an unbalanced manner, that movement is caused by your mind. Thus it is actually your mind that is out of balance.

Now, we've moved a step closer to the goal, but since Aikido practice is done with a partner, there is an additional factor involved. There are many obliging and helpful people in the world, and many of them come to my *dojo*. However, in class some of them want to fix the other beginners' movements, pointing out this and that detail. Often they are completely wrong, and sometimes the recipients of such directions were originally correct. This can be irritating and confusing for the other students. It may seem that the person is sincere and kind in giving directions, but the fact is, he is being very irresponsible. It is like an illiterate child teaching others to write.

Likewise, I see some middle level instructors pointing out minute details when teaching beginners. It is not a good idea to burden beginners with too much detailed information. When you let a child draw a picture, you must not give too many instructions, because this will intimidate the child and inhibit self-expression. She may become frustrated and quit drawing. Let the child express herself all over the paper - even outside the paper and onto the table, if that is what happens. Fill in more information later.

The best dance partner is the one who can lead you in a way you can follow without feeling hesitation or pressure. When you find the mind in yourself which enables you to be a good partner to your fellow students, you have discovered a new dimension in your training and in your life. With a good attitude, martial arts, though they originated in fighting techniques, can become a practice of harmony among people.

~~~

Chapter 16

Don't Judge A Still Picture

The class proceeds with stories, examples and demonstrations intended to bring out the important points in learning Aikido. When the students get used to the technique they have been working on, I introduce a new technique. In this way they don't get bored, and yet are often reminded of the important basic points of Aikido, which can be seen in all Aikido techniques.

The next technique taught at NIPPON KAN is *aihanmi katatetori kotegaeshi*. This technique is basically the same as the previous technique (*shomenuchi kotegaeshi*). The difference is in the attack. Instead of striking the defender, the attacker grabs the right wrist of the defender with his right hand, or the left wrist with his left hand. We call this position *aihanmi katatetori*. The rest is exactly the same as the previous technique (Figure 16-1).

When I introduce this technique, I present it so the students can see this as a clearly different technique. Then I show them that the two techniques are closely related. It is refreshing to work on something different, yet it is comforting to find similarity in the two techniques.

In order to perform *kotegaeshi* properly, the defender should hold the hand being grabbed so the palm is up. I tell the students, "keep an egg balanced on your palm" to describe this. From this position, place your left hand on his right hand and turn to the right side of his body, keeping the egg balanced on your right palm. Keep the palm up. Don't drop the egg! If you turn the palm down you will have to pull your right hand against four fingers, which is not easily done. Keep your palm up, and you can slip out between his thumb and index finger. The footwork is the same as in *shomenuchi kotegaeshi*.

Again, a familiar problem shows up. Because we have started a new technique, the students' minds go back to the original "kill or be killed" idea. Defenders yank their hands away from the attackers' grasps, and force the attackers down to the mat. They were practicing the previous technique quite harmoniously, after I explained the virtues of working together. But now that the attack seems different, students do not deal with it with the same attitude. From many years of experience in teaching beginners, I can tell you that this never fails to happen. Whenever the beginning students start to practice a new technique, they go back to the defensive state of mind, concentrating on an immediate threat and trying to force the throw. I let the students continue for a while before I step in to make an adjustment.

What's so different about this technique? The attack is a little different from the previous technique, but where do the attacks start? In the previous technique, the attack begins with the "H" of "H-I-T", and for this technique, the attack begins with the "G" of "G-R-A-B". In the mind of the attacker, "H" and "G" are the same point. Both attacks start with the attacker's mind commanding an attack. So at the beginning the two attacks are the same.

Figure 16-1: *Shomenuchi kotegaeshi* gives you the chance to protect your back while seeing what else is threatening you.

A movie doesn't start with "The End." There must be a story before the end, and before the story, a beginning. Many things happen to you in your daily life. If you look at them closely, every situation had a beginning. If you see that what is happening in front of you is an end result, it is obvious that there was a cause. Often it is much easier to deal with a cause than to deal with a result. Whatever the problem might be - mosquitoes, flies, rats - it is an endless effort to remove them one at a time. It is best to take care of the source of the problem.

Thus, the "cause," the first motion of the attacker, is what governs your response. Another small difference between the two techniques is in emotional energy levels. In *shomenuchi kotegaeshi* both hands are raised with an inhalation and then dropped with the attacker's strike and exhalation. These up and down motions are closely connected with the raising and lowering movement of your energy level. In *aihanmi katatetori kotegaeshi*, the hands move parallel to the mat, expressing smooth, calm movement. In ballet, strong emotions are expressed with vertical movements, and calmness is expressed with horizontal movements; both types of expression are practiced in Aikido, too.

Your analytical mind tends to register the differences between things, as if comparing two different photographs. What is happening currently in front of us is like a still photo from a movie: it represents only a moment. Rather than being troubled by the immediate problem, look into the cause of the problem and find the best possible solution. I think this is the most important lesson that training in traditional martial arts offers, a lesson which is applicable to modern life.

Let's look at the problem-solving process using another martial art as an example. In many martial arts, a punch is blocked with a strong hard arm and a punch or kick is returned immediately to destroy the attacker. With this type of training, your mind would soon adopt this type of reaction in general. Overpowering or forcing your way would become the only way to solve problems.

On the contrary, Aikidoists never block an attack. We let an attack take its course. But if we stay in the way of an attack, we get hurt, so we move to a safe spot where we can effectively control the attacker's power. We continue to move in such a way that the energy between us stays in balance and under control. This is why Aikido is described as a harmonizing of energy with the attacker.

I have already explained how your mind affects your movements and how your movements influence your mind. To illustrate this, look at the relationship of mind and movement from different angles. I do this by bringing in new situations, by changing the techniques to practice.

Tsuki Kotegaeshi

The next technique is *tsuki kotegaeshi*. This is the same wrist-twist technique (*kotegaeshi*), but against a punch (*tsuki*) to the stomach or chest. First, get away from the punch, not by blocking but by turning aside and grasping the attacking hand. The rest is the same as before. The students act a little puzzled again because of the new attack, especially because a punch seems much more destructive than a grab. The idea makes many students nervous and tense.

Overall, the grab and the punch are different, but until just a moment before the completion of the action, both movements take the same course. The target of the two actions is also different: the wrist for a grab and the stomach or chest for a punch. But if you control the aggression before it reaches the target, then the two actions are exactly the same.

It is my job to help students realize that their minds hold an important key to how they see things. We practice another *kotegaeshi* technique with both wrists held from behind. Again, it is very much like the previous *kotegaeshi* techniques. When the students get fairly confident after practicing the wrist-twist techniques from four different attacks, I tell them to mix the four different attacks but finish each with the same technique. They have to adjust to a slight difference at the beginning of each technique, but the last portion, the wrist-twist, is exactly the same in all four. Both the students and I know that all of them can do all four techniques if they practice them one at a time. But despite my explanations to simplify the practice, the students become trapped again in tension and confusion, because of the changes in attack.

~~~

Chapter 17

"Beep" Living

You may think that because I have written this book I am very fluent in English. The truth is, my English is not so good. This book was translated by Yutaka Kikuchi, my former assistant, and edited by students with degrees in journalism and literature.

I have been living in Denver for many years, but I feel that due to my lack of language skill I have not been communicating enough. I don't have a large vocabulary to express myself clearly, so I tend to listen very carefully to people who are talking to me. Because I cannot catch all the words being used, I depend on other things to understand people. I look at faces and try to see what their intentions are. I observe gestures to help me understand the gist of what's been said. This is like your dog trying to understand you from your facial expressions, gestures and tone of voice. I think this compensation is true for anyone who doesn't understand English well.

It is much harder if I want you to understand me. Since I have a teaching position, people who don't know me expect me to speak English fluently. I have a tough time coming up with the words, especially when I'm faced with strangers, or when I need to communicate over the phone. Friends and older students know my gestures and accent, so they have no problem understanding me. But I feel anxious and reluctant around strangers because they don't know what my gestures mean and they aren't familiar with my accent. When I try really hard to speak correctly, my English gets even worse. If a misunderstanding arises, it gets even worse yet when I try to mend it. This never happens with a familiar face.

How does this relate to the practice of Aikido? You are working on a technique from four different attacks and are having some problems. (Your partner attacks you in four different ways, with both left hand and right hand attacks, so that actually adds up to eight different attacks.) As I explained in the previous chapter, the mechanics of the techniques are slightly different because of the different attacks, but the technique is the same in all four cases.

First, you need to watch and decide which attack is coming at you, then use the proper defensive movement to control the attack and throw the attacker. We've already spent four classes practicing this technique from different attacks, so you shouldn't have any problems, right? Wrong!

First, you don't know which attack is coming. Second, you need to be prepared for any of four different attacks, and that can become confusing. Third, before you even begin, you wonder if you can do all four defenses correctly! In addition to all that uncertainty, you put pressure on yourself to do it all smoothly. The uneasy feeling and pressure are enough to make you mix up your movements.

Isn't this similar to my situation in talking to strangers or on the phone? Basically, people are kind at heart and work hard to do things right. Why do you want to do things right? One reason is that it is better to do things right, but beneath that you actually fear doing things wrong. If you do things wrong you don't look good or seem competent. That can hurt your pride, and it seems that pride has great influence on how people behave.

Many young, educated people come from Japan to stay at NIPPON KAN. They have had years of English education and many of them have achieved high scores on the TOEFL examination. But when they actually start talking with Americans, they seem to lose their confidence, and their voices become very soft. They have basic knowledge but are uncertain of it due to lack of experience. They worry about making mistakes. Scrupulous individuals tend to worry even more. I describe this as "beep living."

On a game show, contestants are asked to choose the correct statement out of four given statements. They carefully but quickly choose one of the four. If the answer is wrong? "Beep!"

Say you are working on a program using a computer. What happens if you enter the wrong information, or even touch a wrong key? "Beep!" again.

Or you are ready to take off for work or shopping, and you get in your car. You start the engine and try to take off. "Beep! The door isn't closed" or"Beep! Fasten your seatbelt." At a stop light, you don't take off as soon as the light changes. "Beep!" from the car behind you.

A child wants to do as he pleases, but always a parent or teacher tells him this and that. That, too, is a "beep!" to the child's ears.

Our lives are filled with "beeps." Of course, these "beeps!" are intended to keep us on the right track, preventing mishaps. However, the "beep!" is becoming a controlling factor in our lives. We don't want to trouble others, and we don't want to embarrass ourselves, so we listen carefully to the "beep!" Trying conscientiously to avoid "beep" generates a fear of it. It is almost like being in a prison, except that prisons have high walls and electronic alarms instead of "beep!"

We wake up in the morning, wash up, eat, earn our living, eat again and go to sleep. Our lives are simply a repetition of these elements. And we move closer day by day to the grave. We have invented languages, computers and sent humans to the moon. It's great, but so what? Are we really superior to other living things? We still live in fear of the "beep!" which we created. If you fear making mistakes, there can be no improvement or advancement.

The important point here is to be unafraid of mistakes. Instead, acknowledge and study them, so they can be corrected. When you become unafraid of mistakes, you can move smoothly.

In Aikido class, one of four different attacks is coming at you, and you have to do something about it. You can move to the left or to the right. If you move correctly, that is fine, but even if you moved in the wrong direction, that's O.K. Once you go the wrong way, you know where the right way is. You can always move again, this time to the place you want to be. But if you stand there and don't move at all, you cannot learn.

Through this training, you learn to quickly evaluate a situation and move accordingly, technically speaking. However, even before that you can learn about your mind: the uncertainty, the pressure, the fear of mistakes. It is a beginner's prerogative to make mistakes. Experienced students should never give the "beep!" to beginners, but simply try to guide them in the right direction.   ~~~

Chapter 18

No Mistakes

I often tell students that martial arts training is like climbing a mountain. First, you set your goal, deciding which mountain to climb or what martial art to practice. In the case of martial arts, you go through the yellow pages or some other directory, and in this case, choose Aikido. Then you start "climbing the Aikido mountain."

In climbing any mountain, you need appropriate attire and instruments. In your case, you need a workout uniform (*keiko-gi*). There is one fact you must not overlook before you begin your attempt, though. You need to know whether you are capable of reaching the summit. For mountain climbers, there is much preparation to do prior to the actual attempt to reach a summit. A climber needs physical strength and endurance along with a food supply and good weather conditions.

When people think of climbing a martial art mountain, though, they want to get to the top instantly, without preparation, like taking a helicopter to the top of the mountain and a parachute down. But that is not the way to climb a mountain. The way is to condition yourself, set up a base camp, and climb a step at a time. If you only look at the top and ignore the process, then getting to the top becomes meaningless, perhaps impossible. Unfortunately, many beginning students think this way.

Examine the summit, carefully plan a route, check all the instruments and tools, move up a step and re-check. If you grow tired, find a place to rest. If the weather is bad, wait till it clears. If the route you picked is not possible, then come back down to the base camp and re-route. It requires a lot more than good intentions to get to the summit.

Aikido practice is the same way. Why does climbing a mountain take so much preparation, consideration, conditioning, calculation and planning? What makes climbers so serious about these factors? Because they are involved in a life or death situation, and they understand the value of their lives. Likewise, Aikido is derived from traditional Japanese martial arts, in which death and life are placed back to back. A paper-thin difference decides death or survival. If you are to survive, not the slightest mistake can be allowed. A mistake gives the opponent a life-saving advantage. You cannot stop when you make a mistake, either. As soon as it occurs, it must be corrected before the opponent can take advantage of it. In this sense, a mistake must become a starting point for a different action. It must be integrated into the flow of technique, much as a climber must alter his route if his way is blocked by an avalanche.

I mentioned earlier that I often see beginners trying to do techniques just right but never actually finishing a technique. Sometimes I see a beginner move in a different direction accidentally and end up doing a different technique, not realizing that it is also a legitimate and effective technique. If beginners had stopped at every mistake and went back to the starting point, they would never discover other techniques. This kind of searching mind is valuable. You are supposed to make a step to your left, but if you go to your right? If you were too afraid of making a mistake, you would never have made the discovery.

Consider a married couple. At their wedding, they vowed in front of parents, relatives and friends that they'd love each other forever and ever, etc. But if the marriage fails, the vow is no longer valid. An important point is whether they searched for a way to maintain the marriage or not. If they were too afraid of making mistakes and neglected to search for a compromise, then they have learned nothing from the failed relationship. The experience will not be a lesson for their new lives.

I have been talking a lot about mistakes, because I find that beginning students seem terribly inhibited by the fear of making mistakes and the risk of losing their self-esteem.

Aihanmi Katatetori Shihonage

Let's move on to the next technique. Before demonstrating the movements, I remind students of the previous group of techniques. "For the last technique, you moved in a certain direction. If I make a mistake and move in the opposite direction, I can do this new technique..." and I show how a mistake can become a different defense. So there was actually no mistake!

People are easily confused, and tend to do "wrong" things, but in Aikido the "wrong" thing is not really wrong, just different. This realization helps students move on to a new technique smoothly, feeling easy about moving, regardless of direction.

The new technique begins with *aihanmi katatetori*, where the attacker holds the defender's right wrist with his right hand. For *kotegaeshi* the defender moved to the attacker's right side, turning outside and back to back. By doing this, the defender protected herself against other attacks coming from the attacker's left. If a second opponent is on the attacker's right side, though, the defender cannot move that way. Instead, the defender grasps and extends the attacker's hand with both of her hands and moves across the attacker's front, under his arm and toward his left side. This tangles the attacker's arm, making it easy for the defender to pivot and throw him.

This technique is called *shihonage*. The footwork is a bit different from *kotegaeshi*, thus confusing at first, but it can be easily dealt with. When you try this technique as though moving on a clock face, it becomes very simple. Imagine that your attacker, in front of you, is standing at 12 o'clock, and you are at 6 o'clock. If the attacker grabs your right wrist with his right hand, move your right foot to 2 o'clock, then step with the left foot to 1 o'clock, pivot clockwise under his arm, and extend the attacker toward 7 o'clock. If the attacker grabs your left wrist with his left hand, then the movements are left foot to 10 o'clock, right foot to 11 o'clock, pivot counterclockwise and project the attacker toward 5 o'clock. I use this clockface analogy often to teach footwork. Ask students to move as they tell the time, and the class seems like a scene from "Sesame Street."

Figure 18-1: *Aihanmi katatetori shihonage* helps the student develop a good sense of balance and timing.

During the next four class sessions we go through *shihonage* techniques from four different attacks. By then, beginning students become pretty relaxed about moving around and executing techniques. They make fewer mistakes in doing them as well. So it is time for me to bring up another topic. Though they move smoothly, all of them move in the same manner, at the same tempo and energy level. It is like watching toy robots doing the waltz. It is like ten people bringing ten pots of the same soup to a potluck dinner. It isn't very interesting, is it?   ~~~

Chapter 19

Legal Size

Many years after I came to the States, I realized that there are two standard sizes of paper. One is letter size paper (the same as typing paper) and the other is legal size, which is slightly longer than letter size. Since then, I have used the name "legal size" in my classes. It is not that the size of paper is important in Aikido training. It's the impression I get from the name, "legal" that reminds me of beginning students' movements. The word "legal" makes me think of precision and standardization. A legal document, for example, is written in standardized language which must mean the same thing to any person who reads it. Legal size paper is exactly fourteen inches long. "Legal size" movements consist of the correct steps, breathing, timing and postures. There are no mistakes.

After using great concentration of their bodies and minds to learn some techniques, new students become accustomed to the movements that they are practicing. Then something happens. They become obsessed in doing the techniques, and concentrate narrowly on the physical aspects of the movements. Their movements are correct, and seem to be more or less mistake-free, but something is missing. I call these movements "legal size."

What's missing in legal size movements is the personality of the individual. Since there are no mistakes, it is acceptable, and receives passing marks, but it is like making robots do the same movements. This standardized effect contradicts the Aikido principle that the mind moves the body. No two people share the same mind at any given moment. Take any two individuals and have them stand in the same posture with their eyes closed. Then ask what they are thinking about. They never give you the same answer. Standing in the same room at the same time in the same posture doesn't provide the same mind. Therefore, although they practice the same Aikido techniques, each individual's mind is different. If a student's mind is not reflected in his movements, then there is no coordination of the mind and body.

When you are thinking of a person as the biggest jerk while trying to greet him with a smile, the smile will come unnaturally and become a stressful act for you, which your opponent will easily notice.

Among my advanced students, there are ballet dancers, a professional level skater, artists, and others. In their movements, I can easily see reflections of their daily activities. On the other hand, students whose profession requires mathematical precision and punctuality - such as government workers, administrators and computer professionals - tend to fall into the category of "legal size." If I leave these students alone, their movements become more and more precise but with no expression of personality. When I see them falling into that trap, I caution them, "You are turning legal size again." I know that these students are seeking variety for their personalities and lifestyles, realizing their routines have become very monotonous. They go to work, sit at their desks, look through papers, sign approvals or return items for alterations. For many people, every day is like a stamped copy of the day before. It is not difficult to understand why people want a little variety.

In Aikido, a group training method is used. In other martial arts that practice *kata*, or set forms of movements, the instructors go around correcting their students' stances, the height of their elbows, and other small details. All the students move in the same way at the same speed, looking very orderly. But in Aikido, that is not necessary. It doesn't matter if a step varies in distance from one individual to another. It doesn't matter if the angle of the hands is slightly different among students. As long as the students stay within the bounds of the given technique, there are no problems. This is not a military training camp. It is perfectly acceptable to see an individual's personality reflected in his movements.

There are many famous classical pianists in the world. They play the same pieces written in the same way. The pianos that they play are the same size. They all have two hands. Yet with all these similar conditions, they still manage to play with distinctive individuality. They use their fingers differently, hold their bodies differently, the height to which they raise their hands varies, timing is altered, and even the way each one feels about the music is different. That is why they are able to produce such different effects with the same music. Individual interpretation provides a great part of the listeners' musical enjoyment.

Let's imagine that Aikido movements are written as musical notes on staff paper. In the third and fourth week, the students are beginning to learn the melodies, knowing which note follows which, not worrying too much about mistakes. An important job for the instructor now is to let students express their individual feelings and personalities.

I show my version of a student's movement, saying, "This is how you are moving." Many students laugh watching me, but also realize how rigidly they were moving. When they don't allow the expressive side of the movements to come out, their movements become small, like withering flowers.

I know some Aikido instructors get great satisfaction from teaching in minute detail exactly the way they themselves move. Making their students move exactly as they do seems a concession to their own vanity. I don't think this is a commendable method. When I visit other *dojos*, I often see all the students, tall and short, strong and weak, of different sexes and ages, practicing in exactly the same manner. If I show a slightly different movement, those students say "these are not

Aikido movements." The extreme example is when students from this type of *dojo* visit my *dojo* and tell my students that only their techniques are correct. This is a very unfortunate phenomenon, caused by their instructors' encouragement of

Figure 19-1: Don't fall into the "precision trap."

uniformity. It is like eating at the various fast-food restaurants that offer exactly the same foods prepared in the same way. The students at my *dojo* each move in a different manner in executing a particular technique. This represents an exchange of respect among different individuals within the framework of Aikido. In order to avoid uniformity and the practice of techniques at a mere physical level, I have my students change partners frequently, or I change the technique being practiced. It is important to keep circumstances changing fluidly.   ~~~

Chapter 20

I Won't Tell You

Instead of presenting the next technique as different, I demonstrate it as simply having a small variation on the previous technique. The previous technique began with *aihanmi katatetori* (where the attacker held your right wrist with his right hand or your left wrist with his left hand). It is easy for me to direct movements when students get stuck in confusion. However, if I do that constantly, the students never learn ways to figure out solutions for themselves. So what happens when your partner sometimes accidentally grabs your right wrist with his left hand? This happens to be another attack - *gyakuhanmi katatetori*. Instead of rejecting this as a mistake, I point out, "If he holds this way, then make this slight adjustment and you can still do the same technique." Rather than pointing out the difference, I prefer to show ways to make the two similar. It is like giving a hint so that you can deal with the situation in a familiar way. I don't intend to deny creative attempts by you. After all, it is your practice time. My job is only to give guidelines.

To beginning students, being grabbed by the opposite hand is a major difference. Some of them may complain to their partners to change hands. In this lesson, though, I would like the students to learn flexibility when confronted by a change of circumstance.

Yet many beginning students prefer to be taught clear-cut details and to be pampered when they are confused. I don't often give such help. This is not because I don't notice mistakes and confusion. After many years of teaching, I know just about everything that is happening in the 50 x 50 foot mat space of my *dojo* regardless of my location. Even when in my office, I can sense out-of-place movements or disorderly behavior. All beginners go through the same patterns and I know when and what kinds of mistakes they will make, even with my eyes closed. So my approach at this stage is "I won't tell you now."

Gyakuhanmi Katatetori Shihonage

In this new situation the attacker has grasped your left wrist with her right hand. If you, in turn, grasp her right wrist with your right hand and extend her arm across the front of her body, you will find yourself in a familiar position, the same as in the previous technique. The rest is the same as *aihanmi katatetori shihonage*. After grabbing her right wrist with your right hand, slide to 2 o'clock with your right foot, step to 1 o'clock with the left, then pivot and throw to 7 o'clock. This technique is called *gyakuhanmi katatetori shihonage*. It is another of the basic techniques of Aikido.

When you practice this technique, of course you might find yourself going in the "wrong" (or a different) direction. Although the movement in this technique goes across the front of your partner, you may find yourself going to the back without thinking; again, this is just a different technique, not a mistake. There could be situations where you couldn't safely move across the front of your partner, and must smoothly move to his back side to execute *shihonage*. We call this type of movement "urawaza", or a technique done behind the attacker.

In solving any problem, you may find that proceeding in a certain fashion solves the problem, but not without causing yet another problem. So you solve the problem from a different direction. This is a typical application of "ura" (behind) variations of techniques.

Ryotetori Shihonage

So you have discovered yet another technique from a mistake! Great! When you keep altering the circumstances you come up with different ways to execute techniques, and you become interested in learning more.

Now that we know how to move in various directions, what if the attack is changed a little? How about grabbing both wrists? Of course, the attacker needs two hands to hold both of yours. Again, this looks like a completely different attack. But consider the advantage for you if both of his hands are occupied!

In my demonstration of this idea, my assistant grabs both my wrists. "Using an eraser, I erase one hand," I say and make a gesture of blowing the crumbs away. My assistant knows the joke well so he quickly hides his hand behind his back. Now you have a familiar situation. What you see is the same as the previous attack. You don't have to worry about the second hand, because the same movements as in *gyakuhanmi katatetori shihonage*. Besides, when the attacker uses both hands, he doesn't have any more to bother you with. This means that you don't have to worry about getting punched. This technique is called *ryotetori shihonage;* it has several variations.

One more *shihonage* technique is covered in the beginners' course: *ushiro ryotekubitori shihonage*, or "*shihonage* against both wrists grabbed from behind." When being held from behind, you must first turn to face the attacker. Slide out to the left, raising your left arm (or to the right, raising your right arm). Turn under the joined, raised arms and take one more step back. Do this as if dancing the jitterbug or a square dance, and you can easily turn toward your partner. Now look at yourself. You are in the same position as the beginning of *aihanmi katatetori shihonage*, except that both wrists are being held. "Erase" one (as in *ryotetori shihonage*), and from here you can easily complete the technique.

By this time, at the end of the fourth week, students have learned to perform *shihonage* against four different attacks with front and back variations, on the right and left sides, a total of 16 different *shihonage* variations. It may seem like a lot, but just for *shihonage* alone, I can count over 70 variations.

I mentioned earlier that frequently changing partners in class adds a new dimension to the practice. I also mentioned a type of student who always gets left behind in the search for new partners. Sometimes this type of person comes to me saying he couldn't find a partner. The fact is that he didn't seek a partner. He could have found one. This type of person seems to be waiting for someone to invite him to be his partner. In other words, he strongly depends on someone else to take the initiative.

Even after such students finally do get partners, there is often difficulty because, rather than trying to move for themselves, they depend on the partner to help out, waiting and waiting until the partner leads. If the partner doesn't lead, these students just stand and look around as if to see what to do. What they really want is more directions. If they make mistakes, they are likely to accuse their partners of misdirecting them. If, by chance, they find a cooperative partner who kindly gives the directions as they like, they move smoothly. If not, they won't move.

This might not be a kind example, but this type of individual reminds me of rental horses at resort areas. (I can sort of sympathize with the horses, there, because they have to walk around the same area over and over with customers who don't know much about riding on their backs. It must get boring.) These horses seem to know who is riding them: with a poor rider, the horse won't move, but with a skillful rider, the horse walks or runs more willingly. It is not that the horse cannot walk without a skillful rider, but that he knows that he can get away with not walking.

Doesn't this example match the type of student I have described? This type of person always waits for signals, and only responds to signals when they are given a certain way. He tends to look for partners who give the right signals. That is why these students always get left behind.

Where does this sort of behavior originate? A computer, no matter how capable or expensive, doesn't function unless you turn the power on and give it input. Without input, the most expensive computer is a hunk of metal, plastic and wiring.

Without input, it is a waste of money. The dependent student is exactly like a computer. Without proper input from someone, there is no attempt at movement. My policy for this type of behavior is to leave it alone. I instruct my assistants to do the same. The students may lose interest or be dissatisfied and quit, but it is not my loss. I would rather wait for them to realize what they are doing by themselves. Some of them stand leaning against a wall and express displeasure, or in the extreme, run to the corner of the *dojo,* sit, and start meditating. They must realize for themselves that all the students in class are doing something together and that each must take part in an active manner. This waiting for input is probably a habit in their daily lives as well. It is like looking at a bicycle, hoping that someday you will be able to ride it. Nothing is accomplished this way.

Good instruction is not the same as always looking over the students' shoulders, directing them. After a kite is flying in the sky, you can stop pulling and running with the string. With an occasional tug, the kite flies higher still. After a few weeks in training, I think this approach is the best method of instruction. I let students find many things for themselves, and I limit my job to giving guidance now and then, like an occasional pull on the string of a high-flying kite.   ~~~

Chapter 21

Scenery From The Window Of A Speeding Train

After a few weeks of Aikido training and learning a number of techniques, beginning students start trying to assimilate everything that has been taught in the classes. They try to organize their memory by thinking of techniques they have learned. I call this the Fifth Week Wall. Most beginning students go through this phase, but it is like trying to remember how many pairs of socks you have in your drawer, or how many clean pairs of underwear are left. It is not easy for an ordinary person to remember all the techniques, but beginners feel they should remember, and feel stuck if they don't.

There are believed to be more than 6,000 techniques in Aikido, including variations and counter-techniques. I don't think I could list all the techniques at one sitting. More techniques emerge when I experiment. When you get to the point where different techniques come out one after another, that is the sign that your training is at an advanced stage.

At the start of each beginner class, 10 to 15 minutes are spent reviewing the techniques practiced in previous classes. No doubt it is frustrating not to remember the techniques. Especially at about the end of the fifth week, this frustration peaks. You have come to learn, but think you have forgotten what you learned. And there is only one week left!

If you are a very serious beginning student of Aikido NIPPON KAN, you spend one hour and fifteen minutes in class, twice a week. That is only two and a half hours. The rest of the week, you do your own thing: work, school, housekeeping, what have you. All are unrelated to Aikido training. Of course, the purpose of Aikido training is to learn traditional Japanese martial ways and to find an application of the principles in your daily life, but this is a lot to ask of beginners. It is not likely that you practice Aikido techniques outside the *dojo*, or spend time reviewing what was covered yesterday and the day before. If you keep thinking about Aikido techniques, you can't concentrate on your work. For now, Aikido is an activity that you do in your spare time. I don't ask you to give up your work and home to practice Aikido. Besides, this type of thing is fairly new to you and it is not easy remembering something completely new and foreign.

Let's say you don't know how to ride a bicycle, but you want to learn. Does it help you to think about balance and steering while you are at work? I say no. You need to actually get on the bike and pedal down a street. You may fall many times in the process, but you must let your body learn.

Learning Aikido is the same way. It doesn't help much to learn techniques in your head. You must try many times with your body to be sure you've really learned the technique. The more you practice, the better you get. The more you fall, the smoother you become. When you cannot think of the next move, you may panic and go blank, but don't imagine a problem and panic about it before the problem is real, or you won't be able to deal with the real thing when it arrives.

It takes a lot of time and effort to learn something new. If there were similarities in Aikido that you could associate with in practice, it would be much easier, but Aikido comes from across an ocean. The steps, movements, words and background are alien to you. It doesn't come with a country-western, or rock'n'roll, or soul rhythm. But one thing is certain: you will show progress with each class. You may not be able to tell, but I can.

The training of Aikido is like travelling on a train. You board a train leaving San Francisco for the East coast. The train goes through beautiful valleys, though the enormous Rockies, across the never-ending Midwestern plains, and on and on. As you move forward, the scenery changes. It is beautiful, but unless you take the ride often, you can only grasp a broad, overall impression.

Likewise, in Aikido training, the important point is that you are moving forward, learning the broad concepts. The techniques are only scenery you see from the train, moving away constantly.

Aikidoists practice simple techniques, complicated techniques, fun-to-do techniques and boring techniques. No matter what goes by, the Aikido train is moving forward, with you aboard. It travels closer to your destination. Where is that destination? That varies from one person to the next. Some of us may ride all of our lives; others get off at different stations. For beginning students, there is a ticket for a six week ride.

Of course, you can extend the ticket indefinitely. Let's assume that you are on a six week ride. It is not likely that by the end of it you will remember everything that you saw. Don't try to perfect a part, but see the whole picture of the movement. When you get too serious about a detail, you cannot understand the whole. Details can be perceived much more clearly later. If, as a beginner, you try to remember it all, the ride becomes more painful than pleasant and you cannot stay on for very long. As long as you are going in the right direction, why not sit back and enjoy the changes of scenery? With this attitude, the long journey becomes much more pleasant and enjoyable. Don't be obsessed with recording the scenery of the past. This is the proper attitude in martial arts training. Don't worry about the techniques you forgot. Work with full attention on what you are doing now. This is the way to progress, and the way to stay on the train until you reach your destination.

It is your choice to get off along the way, but it means throwing away the unused portion of your ticket. It is important to finish what you have started, whether it is Aikido training or another activity. By following through, you will obtain a clearer picture of what you are doing and where you were before you started.

Figure 21-1: Let yourself enjoy your trip on the "Aikido train" without worrying about memorizing each moment.

In this book I describe various stages that all beginning students go through. I'm certain that advanced students can relate to these stages and remember what they were like when they began training. Likewise, many beginners may be familiar with these problems from other things they have studied. Students go through this process many times in learning any new thing. If you feel stuck in your practice of Aikido, try reading this book over to find where you are in the process, and take note of my advice. Going through the various stages of Aikido training will prepare you to become a student who can give good advice to beginning students, if that is your destination.

Chapter 22

Eat Everything On Your Plate

When starting Aikido training, students are interested in everything they see and hear, and try very seriously to do everything I teach. After several weeks of practice, they become used to the training, loosen up a bit, and are more comfortable about expressing themselves. I am pleased to point out the good effects of the new-found relaxation in class. Students spread throughout the *dojo* to practice rather than crowding the entrance section. Students also communicate with each other rather than forcing their way through techniques. But also as a part of this ease in class, students begin to express preferences. Some become more forward about picking partners. Suave guys try to pick girls for partners, or look for not-so-tough guys so they won't have to work hard. Some step out of the *dojo* to get a drink of water, or sit against a wall to rest during class. Some students practice different techniques than the one demonstrated for practice. I could go on and on. Let me say that the *dojo* is a training place, not a social club.

Aikido practice, with two people taking turns throwing and falling, is hard physical work, and there is a new lesson here. Especially during the summer the *dojo* gets pretty hot, and sweat starts to bother the students. Some seem to hate getting sweaty and their actions become very slow. They might be worrying about makeup or odor, again because they don't want to look bad.

Under these conditions, some students don't want to participate in techniques which include vigorous movements. They may not like sweat on their partners, either. Of course, it is good etiquette to have a towel handy on hot days, and for women to have less makeup on, so everyone can practice pleasantly. This is martial art training, so working out in hot conditions is part of the course. Sweat is inevitable. There are times when we have to come in contact with sweaty parts of each others' bodies in order to execute the techniques.

Iriminage

One of these techniques is *iriminage*, which is similar in movement to our first technique, *kotegaeshi*. We'll begin *iriminage* from *shomenuchi*, the front strike attack.

Your partner attacks with a right front strike. You raise both hands, using the right hand to guide down the strike as you step behind your partner with your front to his back. Holding your partner's neck and head against your rear shoulder with your left hand, turn 180 degrees by stepping back with your right foot. If you hold your partner's head firmly against your shoulder, he will be whirled around with your turning motion. When your partner tries to regain his balance, step forward with your right foot again, this time between you and your partner. At the same time, sweep your right hand up and forward, reversing your partner's motion and throwing him backward to the mat (Figure 22-1). This technique, *iriminage*, can be used against any of the attacks used in Aikido. Beginners' instruction, however, is limited to *shomenuchi iriminage* (the front strike), *aihanmi katatetori iriminage* (right hand grabbing right, or left grabbing left), *gyakuhanmi katatetori iriminage* (right grabbing left or left grabbing right), and *ushiro ryotekubitori iriminage* (both wrists grabbed from behind).

Iriminage is a technique many students don't enjoy practicing during hot weather, where a sweaty partner's hand grabs your neck and pulls your head onto his sweaty shoulder. I know it is not pleasant. I try to cover this technique in the early part of class, before the students start working out really hard. Though it is not a preferred technique during the hot season, *iriminage* is excellent during the cold season because it provides such a quick warmup.

Nevertheless, *iriminage* is one of the most important techniques in Aikido, and you cannot avoid it. Since you have to learn the technique, the best approach is to get used to it quickly. It is as easy as going into a cold swimming pool. If you try to get in gradually, it takes a long time to get used to the temperature. But if you jump in, your body adjusts quickly. Once you start practicing, the sweat won't bother you much. It is often enjoyable to see you and your partner printing patterns on the mat with sweat. Maybe the sweat patterns show your personalities, maybe not!

This technique is very effective when executed with speed and power. The attacker is really thrown off balance. From fear of this, some beginners get tense and rigid. Some attackers stand still when the defenders are trying to turn them. With this attitude, the pairs cannot practice well. In Aikido practice there are unspoken agreements between partners about the attackers' role, as well as the defenders' technique. Without this kind of agreement, beginners can never learn a technique. When both sides work together, partners can practice and learn together. At an advanced level, the agreement carries less weight because advanced students can execute techniques with the skill necessary to control the attacker. Beginners, unfamiliar with the timing and speed needed, must cooperate. Learning a new Aikido technique is like learning to write. You need to trace letters and follow clear guidelines before you can write your own letters.

"Move with your partner. Don't resist," I tell the students. Uncooperative students then begin slowly to move. They must be thinking, "Why should I move,

Figure 22-1: *Iriminage* requires the cooperation of your partner to learn.

when my partner is not moving me effectively?" It takes time and patience to become able to move an attacker effectively. If you resist and deny these opportunities to your partner, she cannot learn the technique. Soon it will be your turn. If your partner doesn't cooperate, you have to either force the technique or give up learning. Instead of creating a conflict, students need to learn to help one another.

Either fighting or cooperating can get your partner down on the mat. Which would you prefer?

If you are attacking and your partner is stumbling, go where your partner is trying to lead you and let your partner throw you. Partners appreciate cooperation, and will return the favor as best they can. Step outside the situation a moment and think of two different colleagues: one keeps telling you that you are wrong, you cannot do a job, and he won't work with you; the other helps you, encourages and works with you to accomplish a project. Which type of colleague would you like to have?

Aikido practice is a very interesting kind of interaction. You use your body to teach your partners how they can hurt or control you. There has to be a great deal of trust among students. Don't regard going along with your partner as an insult or a defeat to your integrity. Trust your partner and help him learn the techniques. It is much harder to learn to be thrown than to learn to throw. It is much harder to be a good whetstone than a sharp knife.

The techniques practiced in my beginners' courses have been selected to give an overview of the whole of Aikido training. I believe it is the best program available. Of course, there may be techniques that you don't like to practice as much as others. Similarly, if you are in a restaurant, you order what you want to eat from the menu. If the food that is brought out to you includes an item, say carrots, that you don't like, you won't hesitate to push them aside. Nobody will accuse you of being bad for not eating the carrots. It's your food. You bought it.

Now, think back to your childhood, when your mother or someone close to you prepared your meals. That person wanted you to eat all that was cooked for you. "You have to eat it all." "Why?" "Because it's good for you." The food was prepared with some consideration for balanced nutrition.

The Aikido course is like restaurant food to you, because you shopped for it. You looked, chose and paid for it. But my approach is like the other example - a mother's cooking. I think of a balanced way of presenting the techniques and conducting the course so that you can feel comfortable in the training of your mind and body. It is not the same as aerobics or weight training that you can do at your convenience. In a *dojo,* students train with one another. You need a partner and the partner needs you. You are not training with a machine or by yourself, so you cannot stop practice and take a break. Aikido training is training yourself, but within a group of other students. Working on techniques you don't like, under less than perfect conditions of temperature, with a less than perfect partner, is part of your overall training.

~~~

Chapter 23

Fried Rice

Suddenly the Aikido beginners' course reaches the sixth and final week. Beginning students have shown great improvement. First of all, they roll very smoothly and freely. Do you remember the first week? You got so tense about rolling forward! One student who said she had never done anything like this, and another who moved like Frankenstein's monster both roll easily now. Look at yourself. You move really smoothly with your partner, leading or following the techniques. Some of you have already joined NIPPON KAN as regular members.

Among beginning students, there are certain to be the type who need to compare things, as if conducting a taste test of restaurants. These students buy books on Aikido, read them, and become believers of what the books tell them. They tend to lose the sense of learning for themselves. They say the books tell them this and that, but they don't feel that they are gaining these things from practice. To those students I tell the fried rice story, which I also use when I am invited to teach at other *dojos*.

There are Chinese restaurants wherever you go. They all list fried rice in their menus. However, the fried rice one restaurant offers is different from the fried rice other restaurants offer. It is justly so, because different chefs cook the dish. The chefs are from different places they have different ways of mixing ingredients and spices. There's a difference in taste, and a difference in atmosphere. Enjoying the differences is a benefit of dining out. As long as the dish is fried rice, there are no "wrong" recipes. In fact, in San Francisco there is a restaurant that offers two completely different dining rooms with two different entrances. There is one kitchen in the restaurant with the same chef for both dining rooms. One dining room is luxurious and the other is no-frills. The diners receive totally different impressions of the restaurant without knowing that the two are part of the same kitchen. The same fried rice may taste completely different, according to which dining room you choose.

Similarities can be seen in Aikido training. In the practice of front rolls, I sometimes place a sheet of paper on the mat for the students to jump over. First I use a white sheet, which is close in color to the mat, then the other side of the same sheet, which is red. I ask which paper was harder to roll across, and the answer is the red sheet. The students rolled over the same sheet of paper, so the rolls themselves did not need to be different. It is the feeling the students get from the different colors that made them roll harder over the red side. The same thing can be perceived as two or more different things, depending on how it is presented. In teaching Aikido, I use my own spices and ingredients, just as a chef uses his own recipes to fix his fried rice. I would like you to taste my flavor of Aikido, and if you get a good idea from my cooking, please use it in your own Aikido recipe.

Figure 23-1: Everyone has a special fried rice recipe. The nice part is, none of the tastes is "wrong."

Aikido training is a training of individuals. It is not the same as washing clothes in a washing machine. You must deal with with different individuals with different minds and physiques. A good Aikido instructor knows ways to explain and show what Aikido is like. Many books are intended to do the same, but in the end, what is important is to develop your own view of Aikido. It is not necessary to debate right or wrong each time you see a slightly different way, either of cooking fried rice or practicing Aikido.

Some students tend to be a bit one-dimensional in practice; that is, regardless of conditions or with whom they are practicing, their techniques are done in the same style, without consideration for the well-being of their partners. They may like to throw their partners unnecessarily hard.

A good carpenter uses different tools for different jobs. He uses different hammers for different types of nails. A good painter uses different types of brushes to work with different media and different sizes of paintings. A good Aikido student should be like a good carpenter or a good painter. Don't use the same tool regardless of your partner. I know there are many people who want to do things their own way without regard for ways that are different. You may be one of them. I tell students like this to use a selection of different tools. Throwing a small person violently is nothing but a waste of energy. Use just enough energy so your partner can take falls happily. Always consider the condition of your partners. This is one of the reasons Aikido is considered a way of love and harmony.

In the twelve days of the Aikido beginners' course, you found a small sample of what Aikido is like. It's like finding a mountain and climbing to the top of it. From there you can see more mountains much higher than the one you are on. The highest mountains are not always visible to us. They may be behind a smaller mountain or a tall building or even far away and beyond our sight. Climbing up a small hill and seeing what mountains lie beyond, in the distance, is like the end of the Aikido beginners' course. Though there are many more high mountains called Aikido training, completing twelve classes of the beginners' course is a victory for every beginning student. It doesn't matter how many techniques you remember. The victory prize is not a trophy or a certificate, but the confidence that you won in completing what you started.

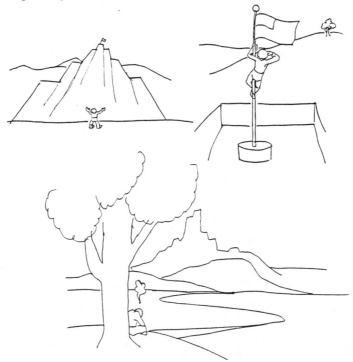

Figure 23-2: What you see in life is often the result of your perspective and willingness to look.   ~~~

Chapter 24

You Are $40

I teach the beginners' course as a six week package. From my experience, I know that this course is long enough to cover the basic outline of Aikido, and short enough for the many interested but busy individuals to complete. Many beginners take the course mainly to satisfy their curiosity. It would be my mistake to think that all the students joined the course because they "believe in" Aikido. To think that all the students will continue their training after the introduction would lead to great disappointment. For many beginners, Aikido classes are an opportunity for them to place themselves in a different atmosphere, a way to spend some spare time. Knowing these facts, I tell the students at the end of the course, "You have arrived at your initial destination. Congratulations! The railroad continues over rivers, through mountains and to eternity. If you would like to continue your journey on the Aikido train, please stay aboard."

I think of the beginners' course as a trial period for the new students. In some martial arts schools, prospective students are shown a few impressive techniques, then told a contract is required for further training. I don't approve of this approach as a martial arts training policy. I would rather give enough time for students to see and think about Aikido, and to find out what the instructor is trying to tell them before they decide whether or not to stay on the Aikido train. I'm satisfied that the students give themselves twelve days to find out about Aikido, and give me that time to properly introduce Aikido to them. When students decide to continue, it is like a bonus to me.

From a business point of view, I should run the *dojo* like this: "Oh, you want to learn Aikido? Great! Monthly dues are $40 and the initial membership charge is another $40. You can practice every day if you want. The workout uniform costs .....". Once a successful sale is closed, it doesn't matter if the new member likes the training or not. But I don't like to put myself in this position. At NIPPON KAN, interested individuals are asked first to join the six week introductory course. This is more fair to both instructor and students.

There are people who want to start training right away, who pay a $40 membership fee and $40 for one months' dues and buy a $45 uniform. But people who jump in quickly also tend to quit soon. I like interested individuals to think a little harder about starting their training. By waiting until the next beginners' course starts, they can double check whether they really want to try it or not.

The beginners' course costs $40. There are twelve classes in the course, so one class costs $3.30. You know how much a pint of ice cream costs, or a piece of pizza. A class in Aikido doesn't cost much more than that. Of course, you buy ice cream and pizza when you want to eat them and you get satisfied right away. But Aikido training doesn't give you that. Instead, the training may bring questions, doubt, dissatisfaction, frustration and pain. If these feelings are as negative as they sound, then $40 seems an expensive waste.

But when you go through the course you find that all of the negative things mentioned are created within you, and that if you maintain yourself calmly, they become very easy to deal with. This can amplify the value of your investment; it may seem worth $4,000 or $40,000! It is you who can make your investment of $40 a gain or loss.

Speaking from a cold business perspective, beginning students are customers who pay $40 to learn something. The instructors should teach what the customers like to learn, and at the end of the course make sure they stay interested and continue to pay $40 a month. But $40 is not even enough to pay for dinner with a friend at a nice restaurant. I don't intend to wheedle and coax a customer for just $40 a month. Cost is of secondary importance. Of primary importance is how you listen to "investment counselor" Gaku Homma, and use the advice to your advantage. The training is not a matter of monetary gain or loss. It is a matter of learning and improving and enriching yourself.

Many things happen to and around you, causing joy or sorrow, pleasure or pain, but how you take these events is up to you. It is the same in Aikido practice. Each of us lives with a mysterious and capable friend called "mind." The mind brings joy, anger, sorrow, and peace. Each individual controls his or her mind, yet we may blame or credit a supernatural being, such as the gods or buddha, or God, for bringing the good and the bad to us. Some of us seek solutions or consolation in religion. Don't misunderstand me. I'm not trying to oppose anyone's beliefs. What I'm trying to point out is the dependent attitude many people have in a pursuit as simple as finding ourselves.

You are the center of your being. All pain and joy that you feel comes from yourself. You are responsible for dealing with those feelings, and find ways to deal with them you must. But you are not the center of society. Aikido training can show you ways of finding yourself among other independent and responsible individuals. In this, Aikido training shares the approach of Zen teaching. Through Aikido training, you ponder many questions, and in finding the answers, you find a different side of yourself. A good instructor gives you opportunities to learn about yourself. Knowing many techniques or having trained in Japan doesn't make a good Aikido instructor.

You Are $40

In disclosing my teaching method in this book, I hope to encourage other instructors to reevaluate their positions, attitudes and approaches in teaching Aikido. Instructors must not be stagnant, but must always strive to become better. This book is like an admonition to myself, a reminder to reevaluate myself and constantly make fresh starts because I believe it is my duty to students to make their $40 and the time they spend in my *dojo* into a profitable investment.   ~~~

IN THANKS

No one finishes a project like writing and producing a book alone, the same way no one truly stands alone on a high wire. It takes contributions of time and effort from many people. I would like to extend my appreciation to all the supportive members and staff of NIPPON KAN for their help in making this book a reality.

In particular, my sincere gratitude goes to Yutaka Kikuchi, translator; Daniel Marion, illustrator; Steve Bousquin, editor of the first draft; Sharon Seymour, typist; Kate Dernocoeur, editor; Paul Roebuck, producer; and Emily Busch, production assistant.

Index

aihanmi katatetori 71, 80, 87
aihanmi katatetori iriminage 96
aihanmi katatetori kotegaeshi 71, 73
aihanmi katatetori shihonage 80-81, 87-88
aikido baby 7
attitude 2,13, 20-21, 47-48, 56, 58, 67, 70-71, 92, 96, 104
beep 75-77
behind 34, 37, 39, 61-63, 76, 88, 95-96, 101
bicycle 61, 90, 91
blocking 74
body 15-17, 23-25, 27, 29-31, 39, 47, 48, 53, 83, 87, 91, 92, 96, 98
bokken 19, 39
bow 19
breathing 15, 16, 17, 27, 29, 30, 31, 39, 41, 53, 58, 83
calm 34
circulatory system 27
confidence 24, 55, 76, 101
control 15, 16, 22, 25, 30, 41, 70
demonstration 19, 43, 71, 88
discipline 20
dojo 1-3, 9-12, 19, 20, 22, 25, 27, 30, 37, 50, 53-56, 65, 70, 84, 85, 87, 89, 91, 95, 98, 99, 109
egg 71
enemy 19, 21, 22, 53, 55-58
extention 20, 28-31, 35, 37-41, 45, 47, 81, 87, 92
falling 43-44, 48, 50, 64, 69, 91, 92
gyakuhanmi katatetori 87
gyakuhanmi katatetori iriminage 96
gyakuhanmi katatetori shihonage 87
H-I-T 63, 72
harmony 1-3, 17, 31, 34, 70, 101
healthy 27

ikkyo 35, 37, 38
instinct 50, 65
iriminage 40, 41, 95, 96, 97
itai 39
jo 19
kata 84
katamiwaza 27
keiko-gi 79
keiraku 27, 28
ki 3, 5-9, 12, 15, 33
kotegaeshi 27, 29, 71, 74, 80, 95
men 58
mind 15-17, 22, 24, 25, 29-31, 34, 35, 39, 41, 45, 53-56, 66, 69-74, 77, 80, 83, 98, 100, 104
mistakes 17, 48, 70, 76, 77, 79, 80, 82, 83, 84, 88
nikkyo 27, 28
NIPPON KAN 3, 11, 47, 53, 55, 58, 71, 76, 91, 99, 107, 110
pain 23, 40, 57, 92, 104
partners 22, 43, 53-58, 65-67, 70, 75, 85, 87, 88, 95, 98-100
personality 47, 50, 67, 83, 84
rei 19, 22
rolls 43, 45, 47-50, 99
rowing exercise 28-31, 35
ryotetori Shihonage 88-89
seiza 19-22
shiatsu 27, 28, 34, 47
shihan 2
shihonage 80, 82, 88, 89
shomenuchi 62, 95
shomenuchi iriminage 96
shomenuchi kotegaeshi 64, 71-73
stimulation 27
taijutsu 19
tenkan 38-41, 57, 61-63
tournaments 21, 22, 43, 53

tsuki 74
tsuki kotegaeshi 73
ukemi 20, 43, 45
unbendable 7,8
ura 88
urawaza 88
ushiro ryotekubitori iriminage 96
ushiro ryotekubitori shihonage 88
whetstone 55, 56, 98
women 49, 54, 58, 95
Zen 2, 22, 104
Zengo 37